where the truth comes out: humanistic education

ROBERT L. SHANNON

University of South Florida

CHARLES E. MERRILL PUBLISHING COMPANY
A Bell & Howell Company
Columbus, Ohio

International Standard Book Number: 0-675-09993-5

Library of Congress Catalog Card Number: 75-168742

1 2 3 4 5 6 7 8 9 10—75 74 73 72 71

Printed in the United States of America

1650719

The Irishman leaving home for an evening at his favorite pub said to his wife, "I think I'll go and join me comrades and talk a little treason." To my comrades in teaching who are ready to join me in talking, reading about, enacting change, I'm directing the ideas in this book.

My motive is to invite people to look at some simple, significant ideas about helping learners develop in high quality, positive ways. I'm optimistic about the possibilities of altering human behavior through teaching. Therefore, let's get on with a look at the ideas I consider as the "it" in answering the question: What is it that every teacher needs to know?

Robert L. Shannon

For Darlene,
who showed me where the truth comes out.

contents

on teaching

the process of
making a difference

Constantly happening wherever people find themselves, teaching is an inevitable process influencing human behavior. Definitions of teaching are unnecessarily complicated. Theories of how to induce improvements in the individual and collective behaviors of people through teaching are erroneously oversimplified. Everyone is taught. This being true, the person who chooses to be one of the so-called professional teachers has the obligation to know what great teaching is and how he can deliberately set out to make his teaching of high quality. Unless he does, the teacher is subversive to the very task he has chosen to perform. Such sabotage of education is intolerable. It is ridiculous to subsidize the performances of persons who do not or cannot function with excellence.

To teach is to make a difference. Teaching is the process of making a difference, and that difference can be good or bad—positive or negative.

Does this mean that everything is a teacher? Probably. I suspect it is accurate to say that everything, both animate and inanimate, is a teacher. Things and people make a difference in people; therefore they are all teachers.

Recall an occasion when you sat in a chair. Perhaps you are in a chair at this moment. Regardless of the chair's style, it is teaching you something. Possibly your immediate reaction upon first seeing the chair was that it could become a place where you could sit. You chose to do so, and the chair taught you that it yielded comfort and relaxation. If you remained in the chair for a long period of time, it might have taught you something else. Perhaps it

3

taught you that you would prefer to get out of the chair. Perhaps the lesson the chair taught was: "This thing is damn uncomfortable and I want out." Possibly the opposite happened. At any rate, the chair was an influential teacher. It made a difference. The chair could have been such an influential teacher that your attitude toward it (and chairs you perceive as similar) was structured for a lifetime. The chair was so successful as a teacher that any future attempt to alter your ideas about it will be difficult, if not impossible.

Then what distinguishes between the inanimate chair teacher and the *outstanding* human teacher? *Outstanding* is the key word. In too many cases, it is difficult to distinguish between performances of a chair teacher and those of a human teacher. Their teaching is astonishingly comparable.

Optimism can prevail. Embellishing the chair is possible. This changes what the chair teaches, as the embellishment is new subject matter. The chair, however, cannot become self-actualizing. But the human teacher can be taught to do something about his own behavior.

Since to teach is to make a difference, and the difference can be qualitative or detrimental, how can the incompetent (bad) teacher become competent? The chair has no choice in determining what it teaches. Its subject matter and how it dispenses this subject matter have been imposed and limited. It either teaches something bad or something good. But the human teacher can learn to function in ways that make a positive difference in the lives of the people taught.

Explicit dimensions of insight are identifiable imperatives if a person is to become a teacher who makes a qualitative difference in the lives of people. What are these dimensions of insight that characterize the outstanding teacher?

> He accepts himself as a worthwhile human being . . . , he feels good about himself . . . , and he perceives others as persons with dignity and worth.

> He understands how people learn. He consistently implements those understandings of the learning process in his behavior with learners.

> He is genuinely *warm, encouraging,* and *nonauthoritarian* in his interpersonal relationships.

He is cognizant of those occasions when he deviates from appropriate implementation of these principles as he interacts with the learners, and he adjusts his behavior significantly in subsequent contacts with the learners so that his teaching is most frequently structured according to these essentials.

These insights are learned, cultivated, nurtured, acquired. Although the process of attaining such understanding is extremely difficult for certain individuals, the struggle is well worth whatever painful effort is involved. With one lifetime to live, each of us owes it to himself to become a "fully functioning person"—a full-blown individual. The potential is there for each of us. Insisting on the right to participate in the process of becoming a free human being who functions at the insight level is a delightful kind of selfishness that ultimately pays off for entire societies. The teacher who possesses these insights will have an openness to experience that constantly inserts into teaching the vitality, ferment, and freshness coming from an involvement of self and others with the world of ideas. Such a style generates new knowledge, new ideas from both the teacher and the student.

Sophistication, savvy, know-how, self-understanding—these describe the real pro in teaching. The great teacher studies learners constantly and determines his teaching strategies on the basis of what will promote positive growth in the learners.

Anything less than these requisite behaviors is little better than the teaching done by a chair. In too many cases the chair may be a more desirable teacher than the human being. Since the chair cannot learn and the human being can, it is indeed tragic when the inanimate object surpasses the animate in the difference it makes. Each of us faces a clear choice. What difference will you make?

what do you know
about you?

A gregarious, self-loving person who has an intellectual life of his own, a body of knowledge that he can call his own, the capacity to be genuinely warm, encouraging, and nonauthoritarian, and an understanding of how people learn, coupled with the capability and desire to put such insights into practice, is the person who can be the outstanding teacher. He has authenticity; he is open to experience; he has vitality. He is an idea man!

Immediately, one might react: "What a stupid description! There never has been a person like this in teaching! It's an idealistic dream." Not so! These are the specific characteristics of the great teacher, and they are cultivated, learned behavioral qualities. The job of becoming a teacher in many respects proceeds in tandem with the process of becoming a person. It is a never-ending process demanding continuous self-assessment. This is the route to excellence.

The single most encouraging fact about man is that he can do something about himself, he has the capacity for self-actualization, he can change. Through deliberate contemplation and evaluation of why he responds the way he does to specific circumstances, the teacher begins to get closer to understanding the bases for his decision making or lack of decision making. He more frequently understands what he is really saying when he says such things as, "That's nasty!" or "She's sexy!" or "They are hoods." or "I can't stand him." The old psychological notion that we hate in others those things we hate in ourselves might help many of us understand our responses to people and events.

6

To be a teacher is to choose to be in a life-influencing business. Teaching is fundamentally a responsibility in human relations, and the decision to teach is a decision to deal in the arena of interpersonal relationships with students, teachers, parents, and the public.

I have described the essential qualities for becoming an outstanding teacher as including gregariousness, self-love, possessing a body of knowledge one can call his own, and leading a genuinely personalized intellectual life. What do these words mean as applied to this analysis of self and teaching?

Man is a gregarious being. He likes being with other people. Rather than being competitive by nature, man as a healthy personality prefers harmonious, productive interpersonal relationships. The healthy personality seeks competitive behaviors that complement gregarious tendencies. Self-selected competition that extends the gregarious impulse is a healthy human endeavor. Competition that has as its goal "doing the other guy in" is an indication of unhealthy behavior. The frequent conversations over the evils or virtues of competition are irrelevant and unnecessary. The imperative is to involve the person advocating competition for its own sake in the process of taking a look at himself and at his motives. He may be advocating competition as a compensation for certain personal limitations. It may be an excuse instead of a reason. Excellence in a teacher requires involvement in the development of positive human relations through the natural gregarious tendency of man. A positive self-image coupled with perceptions of others as worthwhile human beings are the imperative qualities for the teacher who will be authentically gregarious. Occasionally one meets a person who seems to be saying, "People are no damn good—including myself." Contemplate the dilemma of such a person as he is thrust into the dynamics of interpersonal relationships.

Directly related is the idea of self-love. One with a love of self has, as Eric Fromm has described, "a loving, friendly, affirmative attitude toward oneself." Without this quality the life of the teacher and his students becomes a catastrophe of fantastic proportions.

The intellectual life includes an insatiable excitement and involvement with the world of ideas—wherever and however they are encountered. These qualities are not found in the routine collection of courses and credits at the undergraduate and graduate levels of colleges and universities. They represent the authentic behavior of a person who seeks answers to significant questions through scholarship and experience. Such a behavior includes a zest for extending understandings by thrusting self into new and uncertain categories of investigation. It is deliberately struggling with the unknown. A university has been described as an organized opportunity for self-education. It can be if the student who will become a teacher does not perceive his college experiences as a complex arrangement for "getting through" in order to acquire the sacred degree. Credentials take care of themselves if the person is authentic in his behavior with self and others.

So, it becomes necessary to take a look at self. A prime essential is for the teacher to look upon himself as a worthwhile individual. The insecure, self-deprecating person has an extremely difficult time with the job of interpersonal relationships, and teaching is a role that succeeds or fails according to the quality of the teacher's interpersonal relationships. This is not restricted to the in-school phase of his life. Actually, if the out-of-school existence is shallow, rigid, threatening, dull—as perceived by the teacher himself—his functioning with students will be a carbon copy of that docile, drab existence. Regardless of how the teacher describes the good life, he must perceive himself as living it, or life with and for that individual is going to be unsatisfactory.

How do these feelings of inadequacy manifest themselves in the teaching situation? A teacher threatens because he is threatened. He might scold excessively because his life is not one he accepts as secure and rewarding. He carves out a course or courses to teach and desperately resists change. He is the one who becomes expert in responding to change (a threat) by building a case against the change so that his behavior is no longer construed as a threat but a justification for perpetuating the system. These are the persons who stifle improvement of education. By ridiculing an idea and gathering compatriots (equally insecure), these people have no reason to try to understand the new idea, and a stagnant safety is maintained. Fear, coming from a lifetime of being closed to new experience, compounds itself and becomes a condition that reveals itself in a mutually supportive behavior when two or more such people attain positions on a faculty and discover each other. They launch a professional career as obstructors who unwittingly have as their basic motive a quest for identity and worthwhileness for a self perceived by self as essentially a nonentity.

Many schools, for example, have moved into programs of sex education. Movies, resource people, filmstrips, literature, reference books, buzz sessions, and lectures are some of the ingredients common to these efforts at sex education. The basic element frequently by-passed? The teacher! What about the sex education of the teacher and, more important, the sex life of the teacher? How can a teacher presume to educate young people in the manifold dimensions of sex if he himself has an inadequate, uninformed sex life that is dominated by taboos and fears? What will he communicate simply by being the kind of person he is? I suspect the quality of a teacher's sex life has a tremendous effect on his teaching regardless of the subject matter being taught. So what? Recognize it and do something about it.

Essentially there is the necessity for one to permit himself to be open to experience—to try things and see what they offer. Of course, being open to experience includes taking a risk—at least it will be perceived as risk, because dealing with the new in experience (thinking) will cause a person to see the superiority of new knowledge over old (perhaps cherished) notions. The process of meeting and dealing with new insights is threatening, so we tend to build justifications for not permitting ourselves to look. It is possible to spend a lifetime and never permit self to look at what he believes in comparison to a new idea. Abraham Maslow wrote it this way:

> Often it is better not to know, because if you did know, then you would have to act and stick your neck out. This is a little involved, a little like the man who said, "I'm so glad I don't like oysters. Because if I liked oysters, I'd eat them, and I hate the darn things!"[1]

The teaching profession includes a great many "oyster haters," if oysters can be equated with reactions to any kind of new insight or change in behavior that a particular teacher perceives as new knowledge when applied to self.

Another story frequently told about how successfully people can convince themselves that they have the answer and that any further look at the world of ideas is an unnecessary waste of time is a tale about a cello player. A man comes home from work each day and immediately begins playing his cello. Daily, he plays for several hours, moving the bow back and forth with the style and seriousness of a symphony performer. What is special about his

---

[1] Abraham Maslow, *Toward a Psychology of Being,* 2d ed. (New York: Van Nostrand-Reinhold Books, 1968), p. 63.

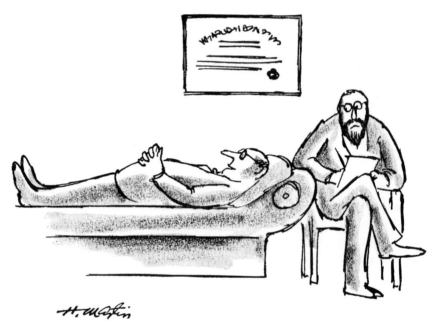

"*I'm beginning to get the real me mixed up
with the beautiful, swinging, legendary me.*"

Saturday Review   November 15, 1970

cello and his playing is that he has but one string on the cello and he keeps his finger at the same spot on that single string all the time he is playing. Each day he faithfully sits in the living room playing the same note hour after hour—totally satisfied with the repetitious sound. His wife is considerate, patient, dedicated, and loving. She lives with her husband's total commitment to his cello, the single string, and his incessant one-note concerts. After many weeks her ability to be patient, dedicated, and loving begins to diminish. Still, she wants to understand her husband. Tactfully one evening she approaches him and interrupts his playing with this comment and question: "Dear, I have listened to your cello playing each evening for many months, and I am curious about something. When we go to the symphony concerts, we enjoy the music of cello players in the orchestra. The musicians have five strings on their cellos, and they move their fingers about producing many different notes of music. But you have only one string on your cello and you keep your finger at the same spot, producing the same note all the time. Could you help me understand why?"

The husband answered without hesitation: "Of course my dear. You see, those people are still looking for the note. I have found it."

In too many instances teachers behave as though they have "found the note." A sterile curriculum, unchanging pedagogical style, and an absolute evaluative mechanism establish a pattern apparently oblivious to the developments around them. They will not permit themselves to discover the educational and personal rewards found by exploring new notes or combinations of notes. There are too many one-string cello players in teaching.

Self-understanding is the vital dimension. With each step toward self-understanding the superficial questions begin to pale to insignificance. Although we never get to the point where we completely understand ourselves, and we will always revert on occasion to child-like behavior or behavior based on what our parents might have done in a situation, our obligation is to spend a lifetime getting to the point where we make mature decisions arrived at by self-understanding and rational analysis of a problem. Perhaps this is the process of acquiring wisdom. As one begins to understand himself, defensive behavior of a compensatory sort diminishes. If efforts at self-understanding are not basic to all human beings, they are certainly the mandate of the person who calls himself teacher.

One time all men on earth were divine gods, but men so sinned and abused the Divine that Brahma, the god of all gods, decided that the godhead should be taken away from man and hid some place where he would never find it again— find it to abuse it.

"We will bury it deep in the earth," said the other gods.

"No," said Brahma, "because man will dig in the earth and find it."

"Then we will sink it in the deepest ocean," they said.

"No," said Brahma, "because man will learn to dive and find it there, too."

"We will hide it on the highest mountain," they said.

"No," said Brahma, "because man will some day climb every mountain on the earth and again capture the godhead."

"Then we do not know where to hide it—where he cannot find it," said the lesser gods.

"I will tell you," said Brahma. "Hide it down in man himself. He will never think to look there."

An Ancient Hindu Legend

the Royalty in pedagogy

Trying to move an entire group of people into the free-swinging world of quality education is impossible. This applies to teacher groups, parent groups, administrator groups, student groups, or protest groups. As the story goes, this is a shotgun approach that might kill both the rabbit and the beagle. In any group of people there are both winners and losers. The winners are the royalty in pedagogy.

Some losers can become winners, and it is necessary to create circumstances in which losers can permit themselves to struggle with the process of becoming winners. But the loser too frequently adopts a role of obstructionism, drawing fellow losers to his obstructionist religion. If he gets a partner, he is in business—foot dragging.

Winners must be emancipated, exalted, privileged. They must be given operating room, a green light. Because a winner is a winner, he will move ahead with people and the world of ideas. Winners thrive on affiliations with other winners. An educational leader who is a winner (perhaps a rare bird) will identify his winners, give them the go sign, and watch great things happen to learners. This same educational leader will have some losers around. He must identify the losers, minimize their time with learners, and maximize the creation of circumstances in which the losers might permit themselves to become winners.

What is a winner and what is a loser? The distinction was beautifully spelled out in an interview with Eric Berne a few years ago. He classified people as Frogs, Goose Girls, Princes, and Princesses.

A Frog or a Goose Girl is a loser. Frogs and Goose Girls respond to situations with "if only" and "but." Losers spend their lives thinking about what they are going to do. They rarely enjoy what they're doing as they do it.

> But to the winners [says Berne] the process of making decisions about problems is a vital dynamic human encounter with life. Princes and Princesses are supremely enlightened people who grow rich, healthy, happy, strong, wise and brave using just three words in life: Yes, No, and Wow! Yes and No are all a winner needs, along with Wow to express the healthy childlike wonder in all of us. Winners are not afraid to savor the present, to unpack their books and listen to the birds sing. Life is simple. All you have to do about problems is make decisions. But people want certainty. You cannot make decisions with certainty. All you can do is compute likelihoods. People don't like that. Paradoxically, the last thing they want to do is know what they're doing.[1]

The "if only" and "but" comments of the losers in teaching sound like this:

> If only I had more textbooks.
> If only I had smaller classes.
> If only I had a free period.
> If only they'd fire Miss Zing.
> If only I had an overhead projector.
> If only I had gifted students, more chalk, fewer meetings, no
>   reports, a marriage—or a divorce—or a love affair. . . .
> If only we had a year to talk this over.

> But they don't want to learn.
> But they can't read.
> But the principal won't let me.
> But the superintendent is a bastard.
> But parents don't care.
> But I don't have time.
> But that's too theoretical.

---

[1] Eric Berne, "Psychiatrist in the Chips," *Life* 61, no. 7 (August 12, 1966): 35.

But sex is. . . .
But it hasn't been researched.

Winners say:

Let's go!
Why don't we try this!
I think we can do it!
Come on in and see what we're doing!
The kids had a great idea!
I had a terrific week end!
Maybe this will work!
Don't worry about the principal, we can bring him around.
That's beautiful!

Most every child knows that a Frog becomes a Prince by being kissed by a Princess. An overt display of physical affection under extremely difficult circumstances converted the miserable looking Frog into a Prince, and the two winners formed a union of perpetual happiness. This took a truly unusual Princess. Her compassion, kissing ability, and social consciousness are a bit overwhelming. She made a winner out of a loser, and both prospered. Perhaps they became a teaching team in a little plastic palace—of course in Dallas.

Wherever such a circumstance exists, revolutionary improvements in teaching can occur. Yes, some losers can become winners, and the menu for their conversion is to have prolonged contact with a warm, encouraging, non-authoritarian Prince or Princess.

But this is an expensive process. Expensive in the sense that children are stuck in the mud while the Princess works on the education of the Frog. Unless the Frog is kissable, or a rare loser, Frogs and Princesses are essentially incompatible. A loser contrives situations that extend and perpetuate his view of self as a loser. He arranges to keep on losing. Not only does he arrange to keep on losing, he also gets in the way of winners, creating hazardous conditions. At the exit of every door of the London underground (subway) is a sign reading: "Obstructing the doors causes delay and can be dangerous." Substitute "winners" for "doors" and a proper warning is given the losers. They cause delay and they are dangerous. Losers must be eliminated or by-passed.

"I suppose you can only be awakened with a kiss."

Saturday Review

October 4, 1970

Therefore, a key to the improvement of teaching is to put winners in the action spots with partners who are winners. If these Princesses identify a Frog or two that can be kissed into the winner's circle, so be it! The winners will be able to make such discerning choices. But if the Frog, upon being kissed passionately by each of the Princesses, still looks and behaves like a loser, the Princesses discreetly (but deliberately) slide the Frog back into the swamp and move ahead in dynamic, Princess fashion. All Frog transformations depend on the Frog doing something about himself. Certainly the Frog in "The Frog Prince" was on the road to becoming a self-actualizing person all the time. Following a period of quite understandable depression after being turned into a Frog because of a previous personal folly, the Frog began to put himself into a position where he could observe a Princess winner's behavior. This took a Frog with possibilities. He learned a great deal about winner behavior, used the understandable understanding displayed by the Princess winner, and made the transition into a Prince. He had potential, and the Princess gave him a chance. The Princess, a winner, would not have needlessly spent many kisses on this conversion of a Frog. She saw the potential, gave him the "business," and great things happened. Had the loser been unresponsive, the Princess winner would have gone ahead without the Frog. Equally important, she would have identified another Prince—maybe many—to complete her ever after story. Remember, she was a winner, and winners have enlightened notions of a love affair.

Too frequently a superintendent, supervisor, or principal inaugurates a massive assault on some element of the school program. The most perennially and politically popular one is reading. A gigantic splash, and the ripples soon disappear. If genuine, long-lasting, quality improvement is what any school situation is shooting for, a global approach has to go. Islands of excellence! Here and there an exemplary situation where something marvelous is happening to children—that is the way to generate quality education. Winners and losers are easy to differentiate if the person making the differentiation is himself a winner. If the school leader is a dud (and this goes from the superintendent on down and from the college president on down), the whole process will continue to be a waste of time. By identifying the winners, putting them with other winners, and providing room for them to activate their ideas, islands of excellence will emerge from the sea of nonsense. If this is not done, the winner will become a troublemaker simply because he cannot wait. In a letter to a friend, Charles Dickens wrote:

> I have no relief but in action,
> I am become incapable of rest.
> I am quite confident I should
>   rust,
>   break,
>   and die,
> if I spared myself.
> Much better to die doing.

Dickens was certainly a winner. A winner can have no relief but in action. He knows the task to be done. He will constantly struggle to improve his performance because of his sensitivity to inadequacy, his commitment to the possible, and his insatiable quest for excellence in what he is doing. Most everyone can recall a great teacher—a winner. He made a positive difference in the lives of learners. Yes, No, and Wow are all he needed. He had unpacked his books and listened to the birds sing—he and all his learners. And what did his learners learn? How to be winners. Princes and Princesses are his products, and society heads for Eupsychia, a world populated by self-actualizing people. The royalty in pedagogy—the winners, the Princes and Princesses— these must get star billing.

WINNERS GO FREE SQUARE DANCE

(Music: Turkey in the Straw)

> Now the two head couples—winners all
> You get an idea and have a ball,
> Move on out, do right hand swings,
> Neglect the losers—they'll obstruct things. . . .
> An alemande left—but don't stay long,
> If she's a loser you'll both go wrong.
> Into the center go the losers four,
> While winners are free—they go explore.
> Winners join hands and promenade,
> Losers just stand and be afraid. . . .
> Give each old Frog a kiss, then sigh,
> Too bad you're not a Prince—bye bye.

on thinking

a thinking student –
what does he look like?

What an incongruous sight! In mid-Manhattan along the Avenue of the Americas where contemporary congestion is the designed arrangement, a gigantic man arrives late each afternoon and stands at a corner. Thousands of commuters pass by. Some look in mild astonishment and proceed on their way; others pass and never see him. This giant of a man stands at the corner wearing the colorful, authentic, tattered clothing of an ancient Viking warrior. He doesn't sing or beg or give speeches. He simply stands there as something of an awe-inspiring figure. What is he doing?

Steel, glass, taxis, people, massive derricks at work on more congestion, diesel fumes, picketers for freedom (or restriction of it), helicopters overhead, beggars, high-fashion models, people, people, people . . . establish the setting in which this Viking stands. Why is he there?

As I passed the Viking, I asked a lady these questions concerning the who and why of this man. Her reply? "Him? I don't know who he is. I see him there every day at this time. He just stands there." She proceeded to cross the street. I continued to wonder.

A policeman at the intersection maintained pedestrian and automobile traffic. He stood near the Viking. "What about this guy standing on the sidewalk?" I asked. The policeman's response to my question was, "Him? Oh, that's Moondog. He don't do nothin'. He writes poetry." Nothing more was said. The policeman focused his attention on "doing something." He maintained the flow of traffic. What is Moondog doing? Is it possible that he's thinking? Who can say whether or not this man is, in fact, thinking or doing nothing? How can one distinguish between the two? What is thinking? How can a person recognize it when he is doing it? We regard thinking as a valuable human activity, but beyond that point teachers have very little insight as to what it is they want people to do when requesting (sometimes demanding) them to think.

How frequently the child in school is prodded to think. Most everyone who has gone to school has had a teacher say to him at one time or another, "If you would just think, you'd be able to get the answer." A rather paradoxical opposite is found in the teacher's comment to the child, "What are you doing?" He might respond, "Aw, just thinking." At this point the teacher might say, "Well, stop thinking and get back to work." It seldom seems to occur to the child that this is a violent contradiction. What is even worse, it never occurs to the teacher. Even though the consequence of thinking might not yield the kind of behavior that is most pleasurable to the teacher, it is certainly a continuing commitment of the educator to deliberately involve students in the thinking process. Since this is true, each teacher must struggle through the internalizing of a definition of thinking that has functional significance for the individual teacher. That is, each of us in teaching must come up with an understanding of thinking that we can actually put into operation in behaving with students.

To think is to deal with the new in experience. If one accepts this as a definition of thinking, then behavior with students, selection of curriculum materials, reaction to student comments, and assignment of daily responsibilities are clearly outlined for the teacher. Everything that happens in interactions with students must pass the test if we are, in fact, interested in involving them in thinking. To what extent does an activity involve each individual in dealing with the new in experience insofar as the new is defined by each individual in the class? Each day the teacher must pass the test, the test being the extent to which he has indeed involved students in dealing with the new in experience. If a teacher has neglected to do so, then it is simple to conclude that very little thinking has gone on among the students that day as applied to the subject matter under consideration. The new in experience that individual children might have been involved with on that day could range from identification of a new girl friend to the mastery of a new play for the football team. It is possible that these two items were in the teacher's lesson plan; however, it is probable that they were not. Nevertheless, if this became the new in experience for a particular child or children, then this became the vehicle for whatever thinking that was done.

Whether it is fortunate or unfortunate one need not debate. The simple fact is that thinking is a troublesome task, and as a consequence many, if not most, people avoid becoming involved in the thinking process. This probably explains why so many people go through life verifying their early notions about many ideas. So long as they can continue repeating a belief without reexamining it, they avoid the troublesome task of thinking about their ideas and dealing with the new in experience. The product is frequently a rather thoughtless person or a consistent thinker. Perhaps "consistent thinker" is synonymous with "thoughtless person."

Another way of looking at thinking is to describe it as being discriminatory. In order to make inferences, one must call upon previous experiences. Beyond the previous experience one must be selective in distinguishing those parts of previous experience that can be applied to a new situation and assist the individual in making a truly pertinent choice. This process is thinking.

A rather specific kind of thinking is called reflective thinking. Reflective thinking is the process of developing a plan—a plan in which you believe and on which you are willing to act. Reflective thinking or this process of developing a plan might also be called the process of anticipating. By calling on previous information that one has assimilated and by applying it to a new circumstance, one can, to a degree, anticipate what is going to happen and the possible consequence of that happening. This whole process of anticipating is indispensable to the development of a plan on which one is willing to act. It is indeed a problem-solving circumstance that promotes reflective thinking.

Jacques Barzun, in his book *Teacher in America,* defined thinking in a pertinent, understandable fashion. He wrote: "Thinking means shuffling, relating, selecting the content of one's mind so as to assimilate novelty, digest it and create order. It is doing to a fact or idea what we do to a beefsteak when we distribute its parts throughout our body."

Thinking, therefore, is quite obviously fundamental to the process of getting an education. Involving students in thinking means involvement of students in genuine problem-solving situations. Rote, regurgitation, and repetition cannot be the formula for nurturing thinking. How many times has a teacher looked at a child and shouted: "Think boy, think! If you'll just think, you'll get the answer!" It is quite probable that the teacher who makes this comment has no idea what it means to think nor what kind of behavior he is asking for. What that teacher wants is the teacher's answer to the teacher's question. Such a process violates every principle that is requisite to involving students in thinking. In *How We Think* John Dewey wrote: "One can think reflectively only when one is willing to endure suspense and to undergo the trouble of searching." Similarly, Loren Eiseley in *The Mind As Nature* summarized it colorfully in this way: "In Bimini, on the old Spanish Main, a black girl once said to me, 'Those as hunts treasure must go alone at night, and when they find it, they have to leave a little of their own blood behind them.' I have never heard a finer, cleaner estimate of the price of wisdom." Schools can become treasure-hunting expeditions for all students where they figuratively go alone, and at night, becoming deeply involved in the thinking process, for this is the kind of educational consequence that renders the recipients happy to leave a little of their own blood behind them. Involving students in thinking is the job of the school. It is a possible human activity yielding enduring consequences that make a qualitative difference in the lives of people.

It's time we got on with the task. Unless an educational program has children involved in thinking, it cannot pass the test as being truly acceptable. What to do about it? Change! Get rid of those parts of the school program that don't make any difference. Eliminate unnecessary elements that do not have the student involved in thinking. How? Such a penetrating restructuring occurs when the faculty of a school focuses on its task. It requires implementation of what the nonthinking, vested interest crowds will construe as revolutionary, and to such factions thinking is, in fact, revolutionary behavior. This is not a topic for system-wide workshops— it is the responsibility of teachers at each school. Will it be done? Only in those settings where teachers have learned to think when they deal with the problems of education rather than to superficially imitate whatever style is in vogue at the moment.

on learning

a sackful ready for carving

We were sitting in front of a living room fireplace, my daughter and I, savoring a moment that found each of us free from anxiety and able to reflect in any way we chose. Jennifer asked, "Daddy, why does the fire make that noise?"

I didn't have the faintest idea. I said, "Let's see if you and I can make some guesses about why the fire makes that noise. What do you think, Jenni?"

The next day we were on the shores of a lake of volcanic origin. Floating with the current were all sizes of grayish, foam-like things. Jenni risked touching one. It was not mushy. Conversely, she found it had real substance. These were, much to her astonishment, floating stones. Where did they come from? Why do they float? What are they called? We had an amazing discovery of pumice stone and its qualities. Then we discovered how easily it could be carved. Jenni collected a sackful to be saved for carving.

And this is what learning is all about—*It is a process, not a product*. Once I have truly grasped the significance of this truth about learning to the extent that it causes me to behave as a person who contrives, invents, permits, and facilitates involvement of the learner in the learning process—then I am teaching in the high-quality sense that will make a positive difference in the learner.

But what are the conditions the teacher must arrange in order to involve the student in the learning process? Human beings are learners. They involve themselves in the learning process, but only under clearly identifiable conditions does the learning become positive.

There is a direct relationship between one's history of success or failure and his level of aspiration. *With success, level of aspiration goes up. With failure, level of aspiration goes down.* If it is agreed that a high level of aspiration is a good thing for a person to have, then it becomes imperative to be aware of the extent to which the learner is, in fact, meeting with success or failure. Applying this principle dictates teacher behavior. It directs planning, executing, evaluating. The result? Significance for the learning team of student and teacher.

And what is the significance of significance? Back to Jennifer and the fire. The question about why the fire makes a noise was her question, in her frame of reference because of the nature of the learning situation. It was a carefully contrived arrangement for operation of the learning process. No preconceived questions or answers (as with the idiocy of the myth known as scope and sequence), only a carefully arranged environment that freed the learner to perceive and pursue what was significant to her. *Learning occurs in any situation to which the learner attaches significance.* Unless the learner attaches significance to the situation, all is lost insofar as positive results are concerned.

And so the teacher has no choice but to be vitally concerned with how the learner sees things. He must be tuned in to the learner's perceptions and regard them as basic departures in teaching. This all is part of the story of teaching as motivating.

How many times does this song get sung? "George is really an able fellow. He just lacks motivation." What the teacher should have said in order to be more accurate is, "George is really an able fellow, but I'll be damned if I am going to arrange the conditions that will motivate him to achieve."

The whole business about the achievement motive has *potentially* transformed teacher behavior and altered the pattern of life for the learner while he is under the influence of the teacher. People can (must) be taught the achievement motive—that intangible something that drives a person forward, that quality of taking stock of one's situation and untiringly, unflinchingly acting strongly to do something about it. Important research has shown that one can be taught to have the achievement motive. How? It happens when an individual is in prolonged contact and presence with an environment that is *warm, encouraging, and nonauthoritarian.* What a simple formula to prove valid. What a complicated plan to implement. Why? Once again the key element in arranging conditions for learning in the school setting is the teacher. Nurturing the achievement motive among learners demands a teacher that can be deliberately, genuinely, quite consistently warm, encouraging, nonauthoritarian. The teacher whose feelings about himself and his role as teacher will not permit him to establish such an environment simply, tragically will not develop in learners the achievement motive. Acquisition of subject matter, development of attitudes, attaining skills—all of these are contingent upon the climate for learning that a teacher can permit himself to establish. A warm, encouraging, nonauthoritarian learning situation is requisite to the development of a positive self-concept. *Self-acceptance* for both teacher and student are primary considerations. Without it the entire learning process is negated or at best neutralized.

So with both teacher and student there is but one place to begin. *To change a person we must begin with people and their perceptions—not with environment and opportunity.* So many well-meaning teachers bring to students a vast reservoir, a bank (too often not a mint that extends and produces more) of subject matter that they genuinely but naïvely expect to "give" to students. The whole deal falls dead when the teacher regards his presence and his subject matter as an opportunity while failing to consider the students and their perceptions. If the student doesn't perceive the circumstance as an opportunity, it isn't.

Why doesn't the student perceive the teacher's environment as an opportunity? Because it is "the teacher's" and not his! Reality to the student might be quite different. *People behave according to their beliefs about reality. . . . What one does makes sense to that person at the time he does it.* A situation that is a challenge to one person can frequently be a threat to the person sitting beside him. The threatened person will behave in ways that make sense to him under such stress.

"Why don't you behave? . . . Oh honey, why don't you behave?" This line from an old love song is precisely the one many teachers sing about students who don't perceive the teacher's environment as anything very exciting nor the teacher's curriculum as an opportunity. Why not?

Because *learning is an intensely personal affair.*

Susi is an expert on how people learn. Her subject matter is boyfriends. She puts her knowledge to work in the process (learning) of identifying, attracting, negotiating, acquiring, developing,

"... And don't be childish!"

Punch

August 5, 1970

© *Punch,* London

sustaining, and terminating each new romance in her exciting, adolescent life. Susi is fifteen. She is my daughter, and she's a sensation.

Initially there is the screening process. Employing a value system that works for a given need and during the ongoing period, Susi picks out the particular young man she will pursue (knowing all the time that the technique includes convincing him that he is the pursuer). This is frequently labeled "need-relevance." Susi uses other terminology. Having pinpointed the next boyfriend, she then employs the intricate techniques that communicate to him that she is, first of all, alive and that he is interested in her. Somehow this never comes as a shock to him. It is the result of carefully calculated "chance" situations as in "The King and I"—"We walk down the street on the chance that we'll meet and we meet, not really by chance." A beautiful illustration of the importance of involving the learner in the learning process.

Things progress until, sure enough, he asks her to the party that he was supposed to ask her to, and things are under way. But this is a critical moment. Now Susi does a careful diagnostic job. Is he everything she anticipated? If so, the next lesson plans take the romance into appropriate advanced study and practice. In well-calculated steps she has, on subsequent evenings, maneuvered him either onto or away from our living room sofa. Assuming he has passed earlier sessions adequately, romance flourishes and he (the learner) has the personal feeling of genuine, complete accomplishment. He perceives himself as a lover.

Soon the subject matter becomes a bore. "Daddy, how do I let him know? What can I do? He thinks we're going together." Now the intricate processes of terminating the romance go into operation. Susi is still struggling with some of the processes, but each experience brings her new knowledge and her understandings become more sophisticated as she participates in the learning process. She is involved. Her involvement is significant. With success, her level of aspiration goes up. In a warm, encouraging, and nonauthoritarian environment (self-designed) she steadily enhances her achievement motive. She begins with a person and his perceptions. She makes some mistakes and profits from them because what she did made sense to her at the time she did them.

Oh, how I wish we teachers, we "experts on learning," could permit ourselves to employ these principles with equal savvy. Maybe there is a transfer effect. Maybe more of us (teachers) need to have (or have had) many more love affairs. Could this be the way to improve the teaching of mathematics or music or Maine?

There is absolutely no escape from the operation of these principles of learning. They are always in effect. There is, however, a clear choice open to the teacher. It is this: Either to know and understand these principles and to use them to create learning situations of high quality or to ignore them and have these principles function in opposition to the formal teacher-learner circumstances.

Since education is the purpose of the school, and one gets an education through learning, and because these principles are the essence of how people learn, why not spend a teaching career becoming increasingly more cognizant and sophisticated in understanding and implementing these basic elements of the learning process? A daily "How'm I doin'?" reflection followed by a "Where do we go from here boys?" is the kind of planning that discovers what individual students are doing with subject matter and what the teacher must do next.

The great teacher has a wealth of subject matter, is a student for a lifetime, and has a spectrum of ideas about how people learn as the constant base for the reexamination of how he is doing. These aren't mushy notions; they are the substance for designing teacher behavior. This is a spectrum of ideas. It is a sackful ready for carving.

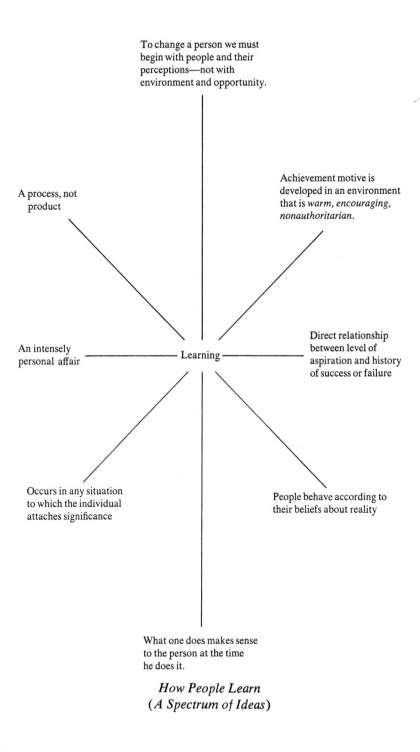

To change a person we must begin with people and their perceptions—not with environment and opportunity.

A process, not product

Achievement motive is developed in an environment that is *warm, encouraging, nonauthoritarian.*

An intensely personal affair

Learning

Direct relationship between level of aspiration and history of success or failure

Occurs in any situation to which the individual attaches significance

People behave according to their beliefs about reality

What one does makes sense to the person at the time he does it.

How People Learn
(*A Spectrum of Ideas*)

GO GET 'EM hAWThORNE

School is simply too predictable. Repetitious instructional patterns, textbooks, unvarying furniture arrangements, teacher in front of the room, windows to the left of students, tablet arm chairs or desks, daily announcements and rituals in the same style and at the same time, bells ringing at the same time each day, lunch on schedule to the minute, grades issued every six weeks, geography after math, math after homeroom. The old myths such as: "Prime time is at 8:40 a.m., and this must be when we teach children to read." "My fourth period class is slow." "They just aren't interested." "The system forces me to cover the material. . . ." On and on it goes. School becomes a drag for everyone. Students find it a regimented bore. Teachers perceive it as monotonous. Principals escape the whole mess by attending useless meetings at which they reinforce each other through justifications of their own foibles.

The school's clients are bypassed while being planned for. Who is the school's client and what is he like? He is a mover, fidgeter, thinker, problem solver, problem seeker, explorer, talker, wanderer, wonderer, tele-violence consumer, lover, and hater. He's a human being.

He anschauungs. Anschauung is a multifunctional term Pestalozzi used to define the functional process by which man forms concepts or clear ideas. The student is a guy who does this whether we like it or not, whether we plan programs for it or not, and whether we create spaces for it or not. He is a being who works at the process of forming for himself concepts or clear ideas. He's really an interesting guy to have around. This being the client,

34

and prevailing styles being the antithesis of what is needed, what can be done?

Arranging for change, perceived as good by the persons influenced by the change, is the fundamental necessity for a successful educational scheme. But school plods along uniformly day after day, year after year, not grasping hold of this reality. Why? We have an explainable resistance to anything one perceives as a new idea. When I am confronted with someone else's new idea, there is a real probability that threat will loom in the foreground and will influence my behavior. In such a circumstance I convince myself, perhaps subconsciously, that if I remain ignorant of this idea, I can justifiably reject it as a poor idea, thereby removing the threat through sustained ignorance.

The result of this resistance by ignorance when threatened is institutionalism. Perhaps an institution is little more than systematized, organized resistance to new ideas. I like this bit that John Gardner wrote about the institutional position in *No Easy Victories*:

> . . . even excellent institutions run by excellent human beings are inherently sluggish, *not* hungry for innovation, *not* quick to respond to human need, *not* eager to reshape themselves to meet the challenge of the times. . . . The institutions are run by men. And often those who appear most eager for change oppose it most stubbornly when their own institutions are involved. I give you the university professor, a great friend of change provided it doesn't affect the patterns of academic life. His motto is "Innovate away from home."[1]

Institutionalism seems to prevail, to the detriment of students, regardless of whether the institution consists of architects, teachers, parents, or politicians. Even students victimize themselves. When students design for students, great things can happen and do. In many cases, however, they paradoxically deny what they know about themselves when applying this knowledge to educational planning.

Once a pattern is established, we lock ourselves in and write reports that build an irrefutable case. Such a process reassures us that we are right. The end result is a national conference of read-

---

[1] John W. Gardner, *No Easy Victories,* ed. by Helen Rowan (New York: Harper & Row, Publishers, 1968), p. 2.

a-paper boys. Cloaked in the jargon of "research," the read-a-paper boys scratch each other's backs, perpetuating the drudgery of school, but on a "statistically significant" level. These protection rackets prevent massive change from being a continuing characteristic of educational life by one crucifying line—"It hasn't been sufficiently researched." Such nonsense. These institutional parasites would refuse to eliminate burning at the stake until it was "adequately researched." These words on witchcraft surely describe institutionalism.

> The history of witchcraft is an eloquent example of cruelty condoned by people whose chief fault was such failure to recognize the possibility that they might be mistaken."[2]

Professors and secondary school teachers are especially successful in perpetuating this "chief fault."

A successful restaurant operator knows he must change his menu daily to attract customers. Certain elements must be consistent, but there must be a delightfully unpredictable change each day, perceived by the customer as quality. The entrepreneur must sustain a warm, cordial atmosphere to retain the regular customer and to attract the new one.

The same principle is implemented in a highly-quality store. Most everyone enjoys a look at current fashions displayed in the windows of a truly good store. Usually the windows are appealing. Perhaps not to our individual purchasing tastes, but certainly to our interest in the attractive, beckoning quality created in the displays. Most significant, however, is the air of anticipation the window dressers create. One doesn't know what to expect except change of a quality sort. The window dresser's task is to deliberately utilize the fundamental learning principle that change, perceived by the observer as good, promotes a positive behavior on the part of the observer. The excellent window dresser is a teacher. This basic teaching tool is implementation of the Hawthorne Effect as a steady diet. He uses lavish methods to let us know he is experimenting with us via new fashions, and we are the center of attention. He knows it always works so he always uses it. Such is the fundamental of effective educating. It is the process of giving

---

[2] Henry Hamilton, *History of the Homeland* (London: George Allen and Unwin, Ltd., 1947), p. 551.

special attention to the learner and being sure he knows he is getting special attention in a special program.

All the "gee whiz" over the Hawthorne Effect began in 1940. There is a Hawthorne Plant of the Western Electric Company. At the plant some studies were made in which lighting on the assembly line was gradually increased. Production efficiency in all departments generally went up as the light intensity increased. Later, as light intensity was gradually decreased, the efficiency of the workers continued to increase—slowly, steadily. Carrying out the same, dull task month after month causes production to go down. But when these same employees are given what they perceive as special attention and concern for their well being through fresh experimentation, they respond positively. They like it. Production goes up. The Hawthorne Effect is the positive consequence of a situation in which the individual believes that he is a part of an experiment to improve his situation and that he is receiving special attention. The result? It tends to improve the individual's performance.

Teachers who perceive their use of a new method as a good thing approach it with enthusiasm. Students, similarly, have more interest and are more highly motivated when they are aware that they are being taught by a new and different method. As the novelty of the new method wears off, the influence of the Hawthorne Effect will predictably decrease.

This clearly prescribes a way of life for students and teachers in a learning situation that is perpetually stimulating. Deliberately, incessantly Hawthorne the hell out of things. Then the menu is always changed. School loses its boring predictability. The essential principle is constantly implementing Hawthornism for all teachers, students, and administrators. No one is bypassed. Even custodians, cooks, librarians, deans, and guidance people are thrust into Hawthornedom. Then when someone suggests your successes as a result of the Hawthorne Effect, you say, "Right! It's a way of life around here!"

ON GRADING

GRaÐes: symbol of what?

Periodically most teachers must sit in judgment. In pseudo-scientific fashion the teacher assesses the nature and extent to which an individual has progressed during a specified period of time while under his influence and direction. With a magical sweep of the pen he attempts to provide some fuzzy indication of the progress a student has made.

Few teachers pretend to have done a satisfactory job with this repulsive task. The mockery of assuming an ability to be remotely accurate in measuring human progress is an ulcerous consideration from the outset. Surely it is necessary for the teacher to reexamine the grading problem with the arrival of every grading period. The word *grade* is, in itself, distasteful to contemplate when viewing human beings in a fashion not unrelated to categorizing citrus fruit. How can the teacher think for a moment that he can approximate reliability in awarding the coveted symbols to a student? Presumably the teacher says, "Assessing everything that has happened to you within the past nine weeks, and within the structure of our experiences together, I accurately place upon you the mark 'B' which indicates you have made 'Excellent' progress."

Occasionally there appears the teacher who expresses confident self-satisfaction in the grades he has administered. He frequently is of the "add 'em and average" category. With the security of a battery of scores representing teacher judgment of the values of previous student work, justification of a mark is considered quite accurate. The limitations of this practice are obvious. Sensitivity to these limitations is less obvious with some of us.

41

Another breed of teacher is found in the Simon pure crowd who are certain that students today are poorly prepared for given levels of work and that there is a need to fail many in order to retain "academic standards." This is an interesting lodge. "How can these kids be passed in this course until they know what I know they need to know?" Criticism of the caliber of students attending school is a popular contention. Consideration of the relationship between teacher self-acceptance and grading practices is possibly of major significance with those instructors who evidence a facetious pride in regarding students adversely. Research has demonstrated a significant relationship between teacher self-acceptance and the teacher's acceptance of students. Surely the extent to which instructors accept themselves as worthwhile individuals will influence their attitudes toward students and consequent evaluations of student progress. Persons responsible for staff selection have a responsibility to assess how prospective instructors feel about themselves and other people. There is a segment of the population that says, "I accept myself as a worthwhile individual but feel that others are less accepting of themselves than I am of myself. I'm not like other people, and I don't want to be. Others would like to be like me but they can't." How will such a person face the problem of measuring student progress?

"Progress is not my concern. My purpose in grading is to let the student know how he is doing in *my* course." Such a comment is also common in response to the grading question. The obvious question then becomes: How's he doing with what, and in relation to what? How do you know how he's doing? Shifts in attitudes? New perspectives of investigation? Newly acquired sophistication in approaching problems? Evidence that he is subjecting personal biases to critical examination? Temporary acquisition of selected matter? How he's doing in *my* course remains a mystery. Now and then a student will say that he got a lot out of a course even though he failed. Does this represent effective evaluation? It is undoubtedly true that many student failures are manifestations of teacher failures. No teacher can fail a student without seriously examining how the teacher contributed to that failure.

Perceptual psychology is contributing knowledge having significance for improvement in instructional practices. A basic principle evolved from this psychology is: to teach a person we must begin with people and their perceptions—not with environment and opportunity. How do each of our students perceive their experiences with us? It would be convenient to assume that we can provide an environment and an opportunity for learning and proceed to show our displeasure when selected students fail to perform to our concepts of "standard." The teaching commitment is to consider how the student perceives an educational circumstance. Failure to do so must be construed as subversive to education in our society.

Donald W. MacKinnon in directing research in creativity at the University of California has compiled, after a six-year study, the characteristics of the creative person. He has discovered that schools may overlook the creative student because, often, he is not a "satisfactory" student. He reports that one of the most highly original architects involved in the study turned out to be one who had been advised by his college deans to drop his study of architecture because he had no talent for it. Many of those identified as creative had academic records which would bar them from today's graduate schools. They weren't "grade-getters" or "mark-hounds" say the researchers.

A person closely associated with admissions at a leading university recently reemphasized the need for focusing attention on the evaluation of students as he described the potential disaster of present-day admissions programs. According to current requirements, Teddy Roosevelt, Franklin Roosevelt, and John Kennedy would not have been admitted to Harvard. When Zane Grey was still an unknown trying to sell his manuscripts, a publisher told him he had no ability for writing fiction. A publisher once told Louisa May Alcott to give up the idea of writing. What does this imply for our grading problem?

Our grading procedures must reflect a teacher sensitivity to the selective character of a student population today. Obviously, this does not mean a free ride. Conversely, it demands that instructors who build a reputation on the number of students they fail should not be tolerated. Perhaps having students experience "F" is a positive contribution to human development. Are we sufficiently sensitive to the negative character of failure? As each grade is affixed to the grade sheet, the teacher must carefully consider why he came to a particular decision. What is he trying to accomplish?

Administering grades is an obligation most teachers must accept. It is an extremely distasteful, inadequate operation. Perhaps there will some day be many schools in which a more effective, valuable pattern will operate. Realistically, there is no alternative. Within the realism, however, is the need to recognize what educators are trying to accomplish. Not a lever, a threat, a reward, or a trophy— we must utilize evaluation as a rough approximation of individual progress. Perhaps we should religiously employ the ancient formula for reliably determining failing grades. All teachers of quality have demonstrated their confidence in these learned words as they assign an "ethical" proportion of "F" grades. Try this fool-proof chant, most effectively performed in a monotone:

> Eeney, meeney, miney mo
> Some poor bastard's got to go.

Some day teachers everywhere will fashion a system that does not teach students to treasure superficial symbols (grades) more than education. Why not make "some day" today?

on values

anything that good
ought to be a sin

Whose concept of the good life will prevail in establishing a plan for dealing with moral and spiritual values in education? Whose sin list will predominate as decisions are made that establish a framework for instruction that deals with moral and spiritual values? Precisely, what is a pertinent design for teaching moral and spiritual values in the elementary and secondary schools? How do people acquire their moral and spiritual values and what significance do these have for educational programs in elementary and secondary schools? The questions are difficult. Answers cannot come from vested interests claiming to have the key to paradise. Solutions must be forever tentative and, at the same time, contribute directly to what the schools are trying to accomplish.

Do the schools have a responsibility for an educational program that focuses on moral and spiritual values? Of course! There cannot be a debate on such a question. However, superficial decisions regarding the nature of an education that fulfills this fundamental task of the schools represent quick cures that sidestep the responsibility. Such superficiality is found in the many quarrels over whose prayer will be repeated at the start of the school day or whose book will be read as the appropriate daily devotional. These verbal wars culminate in blanket policy statements dictating the "get good quick" formula advocated by the winners of the local pressure group contests.

How can educators afford to participate in such quarrels when it is so evident that the religions of the world are striving for similar objectives? Consider these quotations, illustrating that both

47

a common insight and a similar motive permeate the world's religions:

The Golden Rule

> *Judaism:* "What is hateful to you, do not do to your fellowman."
>
> Talmud Shabbat 31a
>
> *Christianity:* "All things whatsoever ye would that men should do to you, do ye even so to them."
>
> Matthew 7:12
>
> *Buddhism:* "Hurt not others in ways that you yourself would find hurtful."
>
> Vdana-Varga 5:18

Ethical Behaviors

> *Confucianism:* "He who loves and respects others is constantly loved and respected by them."
>
> 1:449
>
> *Christianity:* "As a man sows so shall he also reap."
>
> Galatians 6:7
>
> *Judaism:* "Sow to yourself in righteousness till the Lord come and gain righteousness upon you. If ye have plowed wickedness, ye have reaped iniquity."
>
> Hosea 10:12

Obviously, the religious literature of the world represents an enormous potential resource for teachers if it is used to educate rather than to indoctrinate. Limiting the source of ideas on moral and spiritual values to a single doctrine actually subverts the motives of the educational endeavor. A democracy cherishes the individuality of its citizens' religious convictions—including the opportunity to reject all religions.

The tendency of many educators to fashion "cold storage" brands of instruction in moral and spiritual values is probably a consequence of the purposes for the first schools in this country.

Actually, the role of moral instruction in public education has made a complete swing of the pedagogical pendulum.

The primary purpose of the first schools in our country was to teach children to read so that they could study the religious convictions of their particular group. Fear of hell can be thanked for our first efforts to teach reading to large numbers of children. To avoid the old "deluder Satan," a law was passed in Massachusetts providing for the teaching of reading to all children. The objective? Learn to read the scriptures in order to save your soul and escape eternity in hell. The whole pitch was (and in some situations still is): "Become literate so you will know how to work out a good deal with God." As a consequence, much of the education was related to indoctrination into the ideologies of an immigrant population in essentially parochial schools. As the communities became increasingly interested in a form of education supported by taxation, serious problems arose regarding the manner in which moral values would be treated without violating the interests of some segments of the population. Repeated court cases pertaining to this conflict resulted in the complete secularization of public education by 1875. At the same time, technological progress of the United States created another change of emphasis in the public schools. This shift was from values to techniques and knowledge. Perhaps this has promoted a serious inadequacy in the present-day curriculum. Unfortunately, a cognizance of the need to eliminate the inadequacy is not widespread.

Sincerely concerned that cultivation of moral values is not occurring in many schools, certain school officials are construing this to signal a return to a philosophy of instruction for moral and spiritual values that contradicts many of the basic tenets of democracy. Essentially, they insist upon a style that consists of direct instruction in virtuous traits in an abstract sense. Not only are these programs a retrogression from democratically acceptable ideals, they are also an application of instructional procedures that simply don't work. Rote learning is a waste of time in this aspect of education just as it is in any other. The failure to approach values in a functional setting prevents the intended understandings from reaching their intended application to living.

Moral education, even today, commonly consists of required time for a daily devotion. Usually it becomes a planned moment of silent "meditation." In many situations there is a Bible reading followed by rote repetition of the pledge of allegiance to the flag of the United States. The assumption is that exposure to such values of the "good life" through direct teaching will result in virtuous lives. What could be more far-fetched? This is an utter waste of time if moral learning is the end goal of the procedure. Elimination of religion in the conventional sense is no tragedy, but a failure to fashion a way of life in school that is a continuous demonstration of human values is the real disaster. Justice, for example, is virtually nonexistent in schools where the formula for success is to get good grades—regardless of the methods the student must use to acquire those grades. It is an acquisitive orientation—not a productive orientation.

What is meant by moral and spiritual values? The answer requires a look at religion as related to values. This necessitates a view of religion in other than its conventional ecclesiastical setting. Why not look at religion as representative of one's total value structure in its functional, operative sense? James Michener wrote of this so effectively in concluding his fabulous book *The Source*. Eliav the Jew is off by himself, viewing his life and concepts of religion on the day before he assumes a difficult leadership role in the government. His reflection is surely the essence of religion:

> Life isn't meant to be easy, it's meant to be life. And no religion defended so tenaciously the ordinary dignity of living. Judaism stressed neither an after-life, an after-punishment, nor heaven; what was worthy and good was here, on this day, in Zefat. We seek God so earnestly Eliav reflected, not to find him, but to discover ourselves.

Surely the fundamental responsibility of education is to establish the total circumstance in which one becomes vitally aware of "the ordinary dignity of living" and "to discover ourselves." This must be what education is all about.

Morality and its teachings are vital parts of the ongoing responses of people in all phases of their school experience—not as isolated bits of indoctrination obtained by drinking of the nectar of virtuous writing. The responses of students to actual life situations involve moral and spiritual values. A desire to work for the good life for self and others is a part of morality. Morality is not specific doctrines but an ongoing feeling about other people. It is basically what a person stands for in his interrelationships with other persons. Understanding that moral values are primarily related to dealings between human beings obviates the necessity of such education occurring within the framework of the child's experiences.

John Dewey in *A Common Faith* wrote: "At the level of experiencing, the moral and the spiritual are always qualities of an experience." Moral and spiritual values, then, cannot be adequately taught unless they are a vital part of a person's experience, and, inevitably, they are such a part. The question is, will educators recognize this and do something about it?

Every teacher in the school as well as every school employee must accept the development of morality as a constant and primary objective. Moral instruction becomes the way of life of the school and the school community. Essentially this becomes the nurturing of values through the dynamics of daily living. Too frequently the child's school life is far from dynamic. Often it is passive, dull, and boring. What values does this teach?

So another ingredient comes into view—the *teacher's sin list*. Everybody has his own special sin list. It contains that collection of words, behaviors, appearances, and attitudes he perceives as some form of evil. His sin list is what people shouldn't do. It seems as though everyone has at least one item on his sin list that someone else regards as an especially delightful thing to do. Others regard the item as neither sin nor a delight (I doubt that some would accept delight as necessarily the converse of sin), but simply something that has no particular plus or minus value. It seems to me that some people have on their list everything I regard as terrific in life. In the Broadway musical *Guys and Dolls* there is an illustration of this tendency to perceive sin in anything enjoyable. A Salvation Army officer is drinking a cup of coffee which he savors with a special appreciation. After finishing the coffee he says: "Ah, that was good. I can't understand how anything can be so good and not be a sin." His sin list is lengthy; it is a powerful influence on his value structure and on his interpersonal relationships.

It is both proper and essential for a teacher to have a personally significant set of values. The teacher's possession of a sin list is inevitable. Cognizance of the sin list and its influence on his behavior in establishing and implementing an educational program is extremely vital as one functions in a school setting that cherishes the right of the individual to evolve for himself a value structure which has personal significance.

Woodrow Wilson is credited with having said: "The purpose of a university is to make a child as much unlike his father as possible." In the process of developing moral and spiritual values there are many fathers who will quarrel with this idea of Wilson's. Nevertheless, it is certainly true that for a teacher to be true to his responsibility in free society, he must be aware of his sin list and deliberately avoid "making the child like himself" insofar as moral and spiritual values are concerned.

Although religion in its conventional sense should be absent from school, religion is the lifeblood of particular learning experiences. Certainly the historical nature of religion is an imperative aspect of an education that includes analyses of past events and problems of mankind in understanding the flow of history and its relationship to the problems of society today. This involves the world's religions as well as those of our immediate hinterlands. Any study that involves art, architecture, medicine, government, or religion itself will necessarily become vitally concerned with religion and values. Ethical judgments become inevitable as students plan social activities and encounter particular denominational ideas for which they must make adjustments. These decisions involve significant moral judgments and are potentially rich for the development of moral and spiritual values. The Bible, Koran, and other religious books can become concerns in literature, social studies, and science. Much of our vast musical heritage can be seen to contain a theme of values for a culture. Music popular among teenagers is identified as "message music." Its message is concerned with human values. Community holidays for particular religious groups can be the bases for the analysis of religion and its effects upon people in the community. The teacher must see beyond the self-imposed limitations of textbooks to whatever areas of living suggest themselves in order to deliberately make the values of religion an inherent part of the total approach to learning.

It is a matter of helping a child understand his experiences as they relate to moral and spiritual values. This must be understood if teachers are to avoid a tendency to contrive in order to apply a predetermined moral principle to a situation. Such contriving is in direct opposition to the essential teacher behavior for dealing with moral and spiritual values. Nor does the teacher apologize for having an idea. Conversely, he is to be an idea man in the realm of arranging conditions for learning. The situation must never become artificial or the opportunity for value training will be hypocritical and a detriment to the intended purpose. The private society of the school classroom presents situations that are potentially rich in moral education, but the situation must suggest to the teacher a direction for creative action. This will involve discriminating choice through reflective thinking—the most difficult but necessary function of the teacher. Such reflective thinking is the essence of teaching and learning.

Cementing the entire process of value development through an experiential approach is the need for aiding students to generalize their attitudes toward specific circumstances so that the end result will be responsible patterns of behavior. This requires continuing awareness of the place of moral values in the objectives of the school and demands teachers who are sensitive to the potential importance of every situation. With teachers who possess the skills and techniques of helping students to discover and develop values at the right moment, moral and spiritual education becomes lasting, understandable, and appealing when the school is seen as a community in itself. Isolating value training must be emphatically discarded as a solution to the probelm.

The schools cannot justify an educational program that fails to have as a primary function the development of moral and spiritual values. Rote repetition of a religious or moral doctrine is fruitless. Moral life must be an ongoing attitude regarding people, and it is cultivated through an education that advocates learning from life situations. Virtue can become a part of one's value system only by self-discipline. Self-discipline is an extremely gradual attainment that comes about through significant personal experiences. It is the function of education to provide those experiences—at least the deliberate and repeated opportunity for such experiences.

Accepting the principle that human beings are born "morally neutral," with no innate tendency to be moral or immoral, education must utilize the concrete experiences of the school as a community to establish responsible, self-disciplined persons possessing sound moral and spiritual values.

All persons involved in public education must become aware of potential values, both moral and spiritual, in every response that students make throughout the school day. Making these situations real and articulated with values is the difficult but essential job of the teacher. In and out of the classroom, in every facet of the school as a community, students are confronted with opportunities for moral judgments and spiritual appreciations, the ideal experiential settings for learning. In this way moral and spiritual education assumes its proper role, that of aiding students to make proper responses to life situations. The sensitivity and awareness of teachers to the value potential of circumstances and the techniques for vitalizing the experiences to realize such potential is the basis for successful moral and spiritual education.

on creativity

I believe these things are true about people and creativity:

> All human beings have the potential for creative behavior.
>
> Few people behave creatively.
>
> Through education, most people have been taught to behave in ways that are other than creative.
>
> Most arrangements for education in the school setting discourage and penalize creative behavior while rewarding uncreative or naught-thought behavior.

In this essay I have used a narration to expand upon these ideas about creativity. The story encompasses far more than a discussion of creativity. The attempt has been to spell out a life style which establishes a pattern for teaching that's inescapable if one intends to free the potential of people through a valuable arrangement for learning.

g. theodore talent–
creative teacher, disruptive influence

"Yes, there's a Talent. He surely reflects his heritage of Talent." The beaming grandfather, Gifford Talent, absorbed his first look at the new grandson. "Imagine, Gifford T. Talent, III. What a remarkable young man."

"Now Giff, we both agree, of course, that he is an Able boy. He exhibits that intense, discerning quality that obviously makes him Able through and through." Theodore Able, second grandfather of the new baby spoke with the self-assurance he had displayed in thirty years as an attorney. "Theodore Able Talent. That's the name for this amazing child. He'll become the finest lawyer our country has known and carry on an Able tradition for excellence."

Such was the controversial beginning. *Defying conformity, but defending social purpose,* Mother, in her creative style, intervened and found the solution to naming her new baby boy while maintaining family relations. Placating both Grandfather Talent and Grandfather Able, the boy was christened Gifford Theodore Talent. This compromise was more fiction than fact. From the moment of the new baby's birth he was called Giff by Grandfather Talent and Ted by Grandfather Able. Many an argument and much confusion were the consequences as he became Giff, then Ted, then Giff, then Ted as the families met together in questionable harmony. Mother solved the dilemma to some limited satisfaction and the boy became known in the neighborhood as Giff Ted Talent. Nicknames were commonplace for Giff Ted, but he seemed

---

Portions of this chapter have been adapted from test materials copyrighted and published by Sheridan Psychological Services, Inc., Beverly Hills, California.

to thrive on these spontaneous departures from normal behavior and grew into an interesting, curious, creative Talent.

Giff Ted (the Able-Talent will be referred to by either name while this story unfolds) was real lounge material for his teachers. They successfully devoured Ted with coffee on many days when temporarily bored with conversations about the screwy principal, lack of books, careless parents, interfering parents, heat, cold, rain, drought, the superintendent of schools, or the joys of teaching without children around. Yes, Giff was a dandy. What an incorrigible student. The kid was a nonconformist. He was the most skeptical, egotistical, independent character to attend Springfield's schools in many a year. Some called him square. He certainly wasn't regarded as well rounded. Some facetiously, but quite accurately pointed out that Giff had sharp edges. Often he caused real trouble by wanting to follow his own interests. His tendency to resist group work infuriated teachers through the "system." Giff insisted on setting goals for himself. Dedicated teachers tried for twelve years to break him of the habit, but his fantastic imagination continued to interfere with accomplishment of the basic tasks teachers had long recognized as imperative attainments for all educated people. Somehow, Ted seemed pushed by a sense of destiny in whatever he decided to do, and teachers couldn't break him of the habit. They just can't be successful with all students. Perhaps society should be grateful for the successes schools have in breaking most people of behaving like Ted. As energetic as he was, Ted just couldn't be schooled to follow the crowd. He was a real yardbird. Even poor grades didn't adjust him to conformity. He surely wasn't a grade getter. Fortunately, he was a rare exception. Most everyone else thoroughly enjoyed playing rewards and punishments. Not Ted. He just had no discriminating quality. This messed up his values in selecting friends, too. Ted had the darndest collection of associates. The guy seemed to value each individual as a person. The school failed completely in breaking him of these peculiar behaviors but graduated him from high school—happy to have this one out of the way.

Ted spent a couple years in the army immediately after finishing high school. Somehow he got attached to a general as an aide. Coincidentally, during the time Giff Ted was with his army assignment, that general was cited by the Pentagon three times for unique reorganization plans. You might know a yardbird like Giff would fall into such a deal.

The general had considerable influence at his alma mater and convinced both the college and Giff Talent that they'd be good for each other. Giff entered the undergraduate program and floundered through three years of college—not knowing his direction but having fascinating educational duels with many professors. Spending much time in the library, Giff one day stumbled onto the books dealing with the psychology of learning. He read a strange old essay, *The Child and His Curriculum.* This was the day he became infatuated with how people learn and from there gravitated to teacher education. The unteachable Giff became a teacher.

Back he came to join the ranks of those who were still cussing incorrigible students and principals in the teacher's lounge. Little did they know that Giff was about to provide a new subject—Giff the teacher.

From his first day on the staff Ted was a controversial, fascinating addition. Principal Les Turba was stunned and frightened by the events that transpired as he took the faculty on a tour to see his facilities, his custodian, and his materials. Glowing adjectives flowed as Les confidently strolled his halls, describing the carefully categorized elements of his school program. "This room is for remedial reading—my slow readers are in this group. This room contains my accelerated math group. Next we come to a great room labeled GIFTED GROUP. Then on down we'll see my rooms especially designed to house the slow group, the average group, the above-average group, and the non-reading group. But before we see these, please join me in my brand new room, especially designed for the very latest in smart school planning. I've got the tests to be used in identification of this group, the materials to structure their experiences, and a solid teacher to direct their activity." He walked to the door where he reached for a blue cloth which seemed draped over something—as if he were about to unveil a statue. Proudly he removed the covering to reveal a sign in letters of bright assorted colors which read: CREATIVE GROUP. "Yes," Les Turba announced, "we are the first school in the county to have a special program for our latest national concern—creativity."

The teachers chatted excitedly among themselves about this logical new group. Then Giff established himself forever as "the different one." "You surely aren't grouping these kids as creative and noncreative. Why, Mr. Turba, creativity is a human quality. All human beings have the capacity for creativity. It's the school's job to establish an environment where this quality is nurtured, fostered, permitted to emerge. You can't identify people as creative and noncreative and give them different brands of education. Creativity is a quality of living. If schools are concerned with creativity, they've got to set up opportunities for all children to let themselves go, to break away from conformity, to let curiosity and imagination soar. We don't need a special room for creativity. All these artificial groups are so much nonsense. What we as teachers must do is perform as creative teachers. We must desperately maintain our convictions that all people are creative. As teachers we must arouse and reassure the creative spirit in children. Let's excite this creative spirit and let it take form in many ways of expression."

Les Turba observed his teachers nodding in assent to Giff Ted's commentary. Surely his next move would never have occurred had Les operated with deliberation rather than spontaneous action of a compensatory sort. He wheeled toward his creative label, ripped it from the door, and muttered, "This is all the time we have. Perhaps our efforts to accommodate creativity require added study. Let's all report on time when we meet our children for the first time Monday." With the collapse of the Creative Group, school began.

Giff moved along into his first year of teaching with his fourth-grade class the most atypical, cluttered, active area in the school. Strangely, he and Principal Turba enjoyed many interesting times together—some enjoyable, all penetrating. Les was found discussing fishing with Ted on many occasions. Fishing was an art with Les. He made his own lures and could catch fish anytime he headed for a stream, and this was often. "You see," Les emphasized, "to be a successful fisherman a man must have a sort of special awareness of seeing, feeling, hearing, and sensing what the guy in the other boat may not. You have no idea of the thrill I get with the excitement of trying my own ideas out on this fishing. I get completely absorbed. It's frustrating, but every now and then I get one. Then it's been all my own idea. But you know, when somebody pushes me to do it their way, I get all tied up and don't even want to fish anymore. I have to be free to try things for myself when I'm fishing, even when I fail, 'cause I never know when one of my ideas will pay off. Gosh, I just let my imagination go. I've a whole shelf of books on fishing, but I've found out that

I must create my own knowledge. Then it means something and I'm anxious to find more answers. Well, there's the bell. Ted, I'm going to spend today in your class. You know, the more I hear you talk, the more sense you make."

"Say, Mr. Turba, I found an interesting article on creativity. You know, it's just like you've been saying, creativity is made up of many components, and the composition depends upon where you find it." Ted continued, "Creative persons think with greater fluency than do those who haven't cultivated their creative potential. But there are different kinds of fluency. Ideational fluency, for example. It has to do with the rate of generation of a quantity of ideas. Try this just for fun. List all the things you can think of that are solid, flexible, and colored. Each thing must have all three of these. Here we are at our room. You sit at my desk and see what sort of list you can make while we get under way with class."

Giff became actively involved with the youngsters as they prepared to start the day. A young lady had planned the morning devotion. She said: "In my research on people of the Orient I came across some material which seems good for us to think about. You know, I'm beginning to think most of us in the world have things in our religion that are alike. All of us have heard the Golden Rule, even though it's hard to live by. Here is a statement I found in a book about Buddhism: 'Hurt not others in ways that you yourself would find hurtful.' Maybe if we read more about the religions of other people we would understand them better. I also want to share with you a new record. It is a ballet written in France many years ago. Perhaps you will want to think about the different dances which might be done to this music. If not, I hope you will enjoy listening to it. The name of it is Gaite-Parisienne."

While the record was playing, Les Turba thought about the questions he was asked and watched the children. During the playing of the record, children moved freely about the room, exchanging materials, getting books, comfortably consulting with others. Les reflected on the way he and his family enjoy music in their home. Yes, this was much the same. On Ted's desk he observed a quote by Gardner Murphy: "The first principle of creativeness is the encouragement of the child's sheer sensitiveness to the charm, the challenge, the mystery of this wonderful world." "Children are living this before my very eyes," thought Les. "This is why Ted insists on youngsters personally feeling, seeing, experiencing science rather than being content to listen to our expert teachers talk about science on television. These kids seem to dig into things—even though Ted won't give grades. Maybe there's something to this business that he peddles about fostering and respecting the creative insights of all so that genuine motivation will come from seeing one's own ideas taking form and meaning. Is this what school's all about?"

"Let's see your list Mr. Turba. Great! Cloth, leaf, rose petal, skin, hair. . . . You really did well. Let's try another type of fluency. Here's a measure of expressional fluency. This has been found to be significantly related to ratings by psychologists of the creative performances of military officers. Write as many, four-word senences as you can, all different, with no word used more than once, but these letters must be used as the first letter of each word: W_____ c_____ e_____ n_____. You must keep them in this sequence. I'll be back in a few minutes."

Ted soon had the whole class involved in creating plans for their participation in the school carnival. Every student was involved with a personally significant responsibility for the success of their program. It was the students' carnival, planned and executed for the students and by the students. Participation was almost unanimous. They really got involved with the planning of an evening for children—by children. They wouldn't make any money—this they had learned was not the purpose of a carnival. The motive and consequence was the extension of the educational program.

Ted moved back to Mr. Turba. "How'd you make out with this one?"

"Well, Giff, this is interesting. Listen to these—they're all mine, by the way. What could Esther need? Wes can eat nuts. We caught Ed now. What cat escaped next? By George, this is quite a thing. You know, there might be something to this about all people being capable of creating. Say, Ted, don't you think there's too much moving around in here? You should raise hell with some of these kids. They don't seem to worry about the principal being here."

"No, Les, you're the only one concerned about the noise. Noise is wholesome. It's essential. And the whole atmosphere is designed to nurture creativity. It's like your fishing. You said when someone pushes their ideas on you, then you rebel and get uncomfortable—

you even quit fishing. The same thing is true here. Creativity can flourish only when one experiences psychological safety. It's important to provide a climate in which external evaluation is absent. I try to make assignments which call for experimentation, self-initiated learning, originality. Open-ended questions promote this. Hell, Les, a recent study demonstrated that 90% of questions asked in junior high social studies required only recall. One might accurately add that it is recalling stuff that doesn't make any difference."

"Now wait a minute, Mr. Talent, what about knowledge? Where would Einstein have gone without knowledge?"

"You chose the right guy to quote. Einstein said, 'Imagination is more important than knowledge.' Besides, today's knowledge is the imagination of the past, and this is what we study. But what these kids need is new knowledge. Remember the quote from Carnegie Corporation appearing in our monthly bulletin? Here it is on my desk: 'All too often we are giving young people cut flowers when we should be teaching them to grow their own plants. We are stuffing their heads with the products of earlier innovation rather than teaching them how to innovate. We think of the mind as a storehouse to be filled rather than an instrument to be used.'

"Here are two more tests for you. Let's check you for spontaneous flexibility. List all the uses you can for the common coat hanger. When you finish that, work on this. Supply titles for this story. The purpose is to measure adaptive flexibility by seeing how many unique and clever titles you can develop. Here's the story. Mr. John Fox had a vineyard of fine grapes, but animals that lived nearby came to help themselves. John needed all the grapes to sell, so he built a high fence around his vineyard. Next year, when the grapes were ripe, Mr. Reynard, the fox, came around expecting his usual feast. He jumped and he jumped, but could not scale the fence. Turning away in retreat he was heard to mutter, 'I didn't want any of those grapes anyway. They are much too sour.'

"We're going outside for a while. Florida is a great place for entomology. We're studying insects in various habitats conducive to their flourishing. Some students are deliberately removing some elements of their chosen environment to see what will happen. We'll be back soon."

Les Turba completed the tests and began to contemplate the

situation. His eyes wandered to a paper on Ted's desk that summarized some research on creativity.[1] Much of what he read had been repeated by Giff or demonstrated in his class. A few underlined sentences were added insights:

> The highly creative child in a small group often works by himself or is somehow induced by others to do so.
>
> The unusually creative person has a high sensitivity to problems.
>
> Although the qualities in traditional I.Q. intelligence may be some help to the creative scientist or engineer, they are by no means sufficient.
>
> The correlation between I.Q. test scores and creative performance is usually rather low.
>
> When teachers choose, they prefer the high I.Q., low-creative student to the high I.Q., high creative. The high I.Q. and high creativity students were regarded as nuisances, and they were somewhat estranged from other students.

Les Turba headed for his office, encountering Giff and the class in the hall. "Show me your responses to the story, Turba. Lets see now, your plot titles are:

> The Fenced Out Fox
> The Farmer Built a Fence
> Souring the Fox

"Les, these are great. Some of the commonplace titles I've seen are:

> Out-foxed by Fox
> Sour Grapes
> Vineyard in Vain

"You've done very well. What responses did you give for uses of the coat hanger? The idea is to have a number of uses, but also important is the number of times you change categories. You put, to unlock a door, roast a marshmallow, clean out a drain, con-

---

[1] J. P. Guilford, "Factors That Aid and Hinder Creativity," *Teachers College Record* 63 (1962): 380–392.

struct a mobile. Well, I'll have to mark you low on spontaneous flexibility. High in this flexibility are:

> use as a television antenna."
> repair an engine
> use as a belt
> use as a television antenna."

Giff Ted went on through the school day. Just after school was dismissed, Les Turba appeared in the door carrying a piece of poster board.

"Here's the way of life at our school. This poster is going in the main hall. Let's all think this through carefully. Yes sir, a free wheeling, free thinking society will emerge from our program. Look at this, Ted." Mr. Turba displayed a bold pronouncement:

Our nation survives because of its creative citizenry. We must perceive every child as potentially creative and cultivate that potential. Otherwise our teaching subverts our great society.

"And Ted, here's one of those tests I want you to try. It relates to innovation as a quality in creative behavior. Which of these objects or their parts could most reasonably be adapted to be used to start a fire where these items are available: a fountain pen, a pocket watch, an onion, a light bulb, and a bowling ball."

"What did you decide, Les? Frankly, I chose light bulb when I saw this the first time. A second look makes the watch face an obvious choice. I must go now. Our class has invited a panel of people in the community to discuss the situations in Asia. This will bring information, demonstrate a good discussion, and let our youngsters see a good sample of human relations."

"Ted, before you go, tell me this. Your fourth graders are doing all these things. The other fourth graders in our school are not having these experiences. What's the story? The others are fine teachers."

"Well, Mr. Turba, research has shown that creative behavior increases from first grade through third. Fourth graders become greatly concerned about conformity to peer pressures and give up many of their creative pursuits. But in our class the peer pressure is directed to having ideas and trying things. It's just cashing in on their tendency to conform, but conforming to a different value structure. This is the role of the teacher. I try my best not to block creative expression with a lot of artificial standards. It's our class. We're all in the game together. By the way, we've decided not to use those language workbooks. Wait till you see the plays those kids are writing. See you tomorrow, Les."

Les Turba headed for his car. Tonight he was going after a bass he'd heard rumors about. He's so confident about his own judgment and evaluations of his own work that he discounts criticisms of others and seems to disparage their judgment. Who knows, maybe the guy is one of those creative people.

on individual differences

wheRe the tRuth comes out

Pete sat in the plush lobby of the Heavenly Hilton, absorbing the excitement of the astonishing celestial gathering. At last he was in the midst of the first A.C.E.H. Conference since formal admission to Heaven. Perhaps going through the battery of admissions tests would prove to have been worth all the anguish it had caused Pete. He reflected on the experience. He had sweat through the G.R.E. (General Relations with Everyone), N.T.E. (Non-Teaching Enthusiasms), a 3.0 average for 60 credits of upper-division behavior at Pearly Gates U. (Extension Division at Purgatory), and testimonials from ten former students who had preceded him into paradise. This became a rigorous investigation of many qualities he had not heretofore had tested. Having the measurements be consistently concerned with personal, human qualities such as integrity and principles of human behavior was a startling new experience. It was heavenly.

Pete had been ready to state concise definitions of those earthly indispensables: normal curve, mean, median, mode, seven cardinal principles, and Carnegie units. To demonstrate his contemporary insights, he had planned to say magic words like ungraded, team teaching, television, and flexible. None of this was requested.

Admissions officials (a staff made up of experts who had served this function at universities all over earth and would now spend eternity with their concept of the good life in an admissions office) had punched dozens of H.B.M. cards and had rapturously sorted, counted, ranked, duplicated, and filed them for eternity. Admissions were at a new high because of several wars, selected riots,

71

and excellent cooperation from the automobile industry. The consequence was an extremely high-spirited admissions office. This spirit facilitated Pete's clearance, so he had arrived at Hilton convention headquarters in time for early registration at A.C.E.H. (All Children are Exceptional in Heaven). This contrasts favorably with the earth organization A.C.E.I. (Average Children Exist in Imaginations).

With the inevitable name card in vogue in heaven, he accepted the billboard role and affixed his label at the rakish angle that designates one with many hash marks for convention attendance. The name card angle was only a compensation for a terrific inferiority that Pete felt in this setting. He was genuinely and uncomfortably awed by the prospects of what he expected. He anticipated at least a look at and possibly a personal confrontation with the greatest figures in the history of education.

An impact of life (or whatever it is) in heaven was the absence of any common style and the presence of many styles of dress. Fortunately, Pete had experienced the life adjustment curriculum in his prior educational setting, so he was (he surmised) able to handle heaven adjustment smoothly (assuming transfer of training occurred). He longed for an opportunity to meet with earth educators to sensitize them to the essentiality of adding this dimension to the purposes and subsequent programs in the life adjustment series. A unit on Understanding Heaven could be properly included in the scope and sequence by putting it in for all students during May of the sixth year at every elementary school. Working out resource people and field experiences could present certain obstacles, but these were not insurmountable.

Pete had passed on (or up, or somewhere) during the single-breasted, three-button suit period, so he regarded this as an appropriate style for himself. Others seemed oblivious to style. He got the impression that too many of them were on tenure and expected to be there an eternity. This contemplation was abruptly disrupted by a peculiar man dressed in what Pete saw as a sheet.

"Socrates is my name; I don't believe we've met at previous A.C.E.H. sessions. Perhaps you're new." What could Pete say? His first contact at the heavenly conclave, and he is meeting "The Different One" face to face.

Years of conventioneering paid off, however, and Pete responded with lobby expertise in spite of an obvious awe: "Peter is my name, Jim Peter. Yes, I was just cleared by the selections committee in time to get here and am I glad to meet you. I need to discuss some basic questions with you if you have time."

"Of course I have time. That's why I'm here. Jim Peter. Any relation to the fellow we call the Saint? He's a mighty good man around here. Actually, he's the convention director for this and all other meetings like this one."

"I don't know if we're related. He was in a planning meeting when I was admitted so we didn't meet. I understand that there's not another one like St. Peter. He's different."

"Well," Socrates asked, "I wonder how many people you've met who are anything but different? Say, I'm on my way to meet some friends in the bar. Come along. You'll enjoy it." Socrates opened the door of the Starlight Ballroom. It was jammed with several thousand head nodders—all seemingly in mass agreement. The speaker was having a great time. Pete hesitated long enough to absorb portions of this astonishing speech. . . .

"Again let me emphasize the delightful academic consequences of homogeneous grouping. My monumental study done in 1893 and since replicated with various modifications that tend to validate my fundamental research which continues to be quoted in the literature reveals that when students are grouped according to results of carefully selected instruments that yield I.Q., reading achievement, chronological age, religious affiliation, aptitude, and hair color, it is conveniently possible to upgrade academic achievement to a statistically significant degree when such achievement is measured by better grades in comparison with schools where students do not eat breakfast or attend symphony concerts. These data provide incontrovertible evidence of the. . . ."

Bewildered, disappointed, Pete staggered away from the closing door as the homogeneous disciple droned on. "This can't be. How can that bit of idiocy gain a packed audience? I thought I'd heard from those birds for the last time."

Socrates indicated understanding and restated Pete's question. "How can heaven, the paradise of free expression and identity sanction an assumption that human beings can be homogeneous?"

Pete accepted the counter question and found himself formulating a response that now seemed obvious. "It couldn't be any other way," Pete revealed. "This behavior is everything these people could ask for. They spent a lifetime convincing themselves of the validity of this simple solution to educational planning. Now they have elected to spend eternity reaffirming this stand for themselves."

"Precisely." Socrates was relishing Pete's responses. "You see, Pete, Dr. Search has given essentially the same speech for the last seventy years at every convention for educators that is conducted in heaven. The auditorium is always packed with the same souls, plus an additional population of non-thinking, panacea seekers that join us as our population inevitably expands. Between occasions, when he delivers this speech on the delights of homogeneous grouping, Dr. Search is assigned to teaching responsibilities with the extension division. Once a week St. Peter tells him to go to hell, so he happily reports in hell for a three-hour class he teaches. It's a course on grouping for individual differences. Actually, he's sort of in heaven when he's in hell, because his class is composed of an almost perfect homogeneous group. All students are exactly alike. Same I.Q., same academic backgrounds, mutual interests, identical physical features, carbon copies insofar as clothing is concerned (they prefer an intense red uniform), total agreement on all matters. We get a terrific kick out of the one deviation that frustrates poor Dr. Search in this class. You see, St. Peter had to coordinate the establishment of this class through the administration in hell. He has had a devil of a time getting through the central office bureaucrats. You can appreciate the problem if you understand that all school administrative personnel go to hell—without deviation. Consequently it's almost impossible to get anything done down there. Well, in order to get through this devilment, St. Peter had to make one concession. There are, of course, thirty students in Dr. Search's class, all identical, with this one exception. Half of them are male and the other half are female. Fifteen females, and each carbon copy . . . wild as the devil. They behave exactly alike. It's a little sad I guess, cause old Search is really frustrated with this difference. Sometimes I think St. Peter deliberately arranged this as a kind of periodic purgatory for Search to make up for what he did to children through his influential ballyhoo on homogenized people while he was on earth. Other than the extension course, Dr. Search is having an ideal eternity for himself. He gripes a lot about it, but that's really part of his eternal happiness. Complaining seems to be somehow personally rewarding. Well, let's see who is in the bar. Great! There are John and Maria. Just look at that. Maria, excited, anxious, demanding—John sort of looking into nowhere, just as though he'd never had a thought in his life. Come on, Pete."

They maneuvered through many tables and reached a large booth in the corner where a man and woman were sitting. Socrates handled the introductions. "John, Maria, you'll enjoy knowing a new man that I think will add many provocative questions for our contemplations. This is Pete. Jim Peter is the proper name, I guess. Pete, this is Maria Montessori and John Dewey."

Appropriate greetings were completed, and Pete insisted on obtaining the first bottle for their table. An angelic creature brought the bottle, and her appearance seemed to relax Pete, even in this audience. He made a mental note to find out more about her. This eternity idea surely seemed promising.

Thirty minutes of conviviality seemed to get Pete to the point where he was ready to pose a question that had troubled him at the time he made a sudden departure from earth. He spoke to the three famous educators with a self assurance he had heretofore never experienced. "Just before leaving earth I was asked to give a talk at a meeting for elementary teachers. The title they gave me for the speech was this: 'When They Are Different.' The 'they' that conference planners had in mind was, very probably, children. The whole thing refers to the kind of school experience that should be designed for children when they are different. I'm wondering how you would respond to the responsibility."

Socrates was the first to react. "Before we make any comments, let's try a little experiment. Let's stop several people who pass this booth and ask them who they are and how their school experiences provided for students who were different. Let's start with the fellow smoking the big cigar. Pete, you do the questioning."

From the confidence acquired from continued enthusiasm for the truth serum Socrates so ably selected, Pete had no reservations as he spoke to the jovial man who had reached their table. "Sir, I'm Jim Peter. I wonder if you would mind discussing recollections of your school experiences and how the teachers handled students who were different."

"Not at all. It seems like that's one of my responsibilities around here—answering questions asked by a man called Peter. Churchill's my name, Winston Churchill. I'm sort of a newcomer to this place. It's as I anticipated. I'm spending a good deal of time painting, and I've found millions of exciting new celestial colors. If I'm to make a bit of a speech, I'll need a drink. You can't make a speech on iced water. What to do when they are different? Give them every chance to be such. Don't do what my teachers did. Of course, how could I feel otherwise. I was regarded by my teachers as a very poor student. I am surprised that in my later life I became so experienced in taking degrees when as a schoolboy I was so bad at passing examinations. In fact, one might say that no one ever passed so few examinations and received so many degrees. Now for another brandy. I neither want it nor need it, but I should think it pretty hazardous to interfere with the ineradicable habit of a lifetime. Here's Adlai Stevenson coming in. Adlai, you were regarded as the most cultured of political candidates. Let's hear your views on what educators can do with students who are different."

"Gentlemen, I was such a mediocre student in high school that I had to be sent to a prep school before I was admitted to Princeton. My college record was undistinguished, and so were my two years at Harvard Law School. Actually I finally finished law school at Northwestern. Perhaps I'm the wrong person to ask. I just wasn't a very normal case. Churchill and I must go, but Jack Kennedy should have some answers. Let me send him over."

Stevenson hesitated at an adjacent table, and the two men who were there got up and came to our booth. Pete was introduced to Kennedy and his friend Albert Einstein. The question was put to them. Kennedy was the first to speak.

"It's hard to judge how much my formal education mattered. I spent only one year at a Catholic school in Connecticut. Then I went on to Choate, which I disliked heartily. I finished only slightly above the middle of my class. I'm not sure how much this provides as an answer to your question. Perhaps I was, as you say, a student that was different. I remember just before we were married Jacqueline asked me what I considered to be my best and worst qualities. I said, in my opinion, my best quality is curiosity and my worst is irritability. By irritability I mean impatience with the boring, the commonplace, the mediocre. By curiosity I mean a hunger for experience which causes one to demand that life be concentrated, vivid, and full. Because of what I was asked to do in school, I found it irritable—a place where there were few opportunities to pursue this style of curiosity. Maybe a school for the child who is different would be cognizant of one's best and worst qualities and use these insights for positive emergence of the individual."

Einstein spoke up at this point: "This is precisely the need—nurture the individual. How can a person be other than different? I say this, in answer to your question. When they are different: Let every man be respected as an individual and no man idolized."

Pete broke into the conversation: "So much of this seems to relate to how we see ourselves. Kennedy called himself a mediocre student. So did Stevenson. Churchill's teachers regarded him as a poor student. I've asked you to talk about a program for children who are supposedly different. I wonder what I should understand about myself that seems to compel me to want to categorize students? I'm sensitive to this because of this book by Krishnamurti, *Education and the Significance of Life,* that I picked up in the Hilton book store. He wrote, 'In order to help the child to be intelligent we have to break down within ourselves those hindrances which make us dull and thoughtless.' Perhaps I'm asking a dull and thoughtless question about a dull and thoughtless school program that sees human beings as other than different."

Socrates did not reject Pete's comment but redirected the conversants. "Now back to our commitment to ask the question of persons who pass our table. Here is a tousle-haired deviant. Pete, meet Frank Lloyd Wright. Frank, what's your reaction to the question of what teachers can do when students are different?"

"This is obvious. How else can students be? Of course, I've seen some pathetic architects who studied under me—not all of them, of course, but many of them who denied themselves their creative competences and became "Wright School" architects. These persons, for various motives, deliberately endeavored to deny their own delightful differences in order to become a 'me,' and that wasn't worth becoming in the first place. What to do when they are different? Get out of the way! Take this fellow." Wright displayed a book he was carrying and continued, "Buckminster Fuller hasn't joined us yet, but copies of his book *Freeing the Scholar to Return to His Studies* are around so he's probably being given some advanced consideration. Fuller, as you know, created what he calls the geodesic dome. It's a fantastic architectural revolution. Fuller created the dome—only because he was different and in spite of his education. As Buckminster Fuller tells it, he was fired from Harvard twice while an undergraduate student and ultimately invited back as a visiting lecturer. This man refers to himself as a 'random element.' What higher praise could a man receive than to be categorized as a 'random element.' The different ones are the ones that make a difference. I've got to get on my way. With my continued dedication to the principle that form must follow function, I've been having a great time with a new problem. St. Peter seems to want us to rethink the whole pearly-gate concept. At the same time, he feels a real obligation to those who want to sustain the aesthetics of tradition. I'd surely like to visit with Buckminster Fuller on this problem."

With that, Wright disappeared through a door that was immediately filled with a jovial, boisterous fellow whose attentions were casually dedicated to the two beautiful women devotedly clinging to his every expression. "Jean, come and join us." The two lovely ladies seemed to assume a role of polite withdrawal from the man's attentions as he left them to join Socrates, Pete, Dewey, and Maria Montessori. "Jean, let me introduce you to a new man who is confronting us with a question you'll enjoy. This is Jim Peter—call him Pete. Pete, shake hands with Jean Rousseau. Jean, you'll remember, shocked educators around 1750 with a different conception of schooling. He is said to have written the Declaration of Independence for Children. His strange behavior caused some real problems on earth, but here he has found paradise for these different ideas."

"Yes," Pete quipped, "I see you are implementing your ideas on the education of women. They are beautiful."

"And dependable," Rousseau added. "You will recall that I insist the proper education for women is that which is necessary to enable them to serve the needs of men. The two who are with me today are well educated. Heaven is heaven. What's the question we're discussing?"

Pete stated the question again. "What do you do in an educational setting when they are different—the students, I mean?"

Another stranger had sat down with the group as Pete was talking, but the man said nothing. The new person studied Rousseau carefully and listened to his response to Pete's question. Rousseau said, "Every man is born with a character, abilities, and talents peculiar to him. It is in vain, then, to claim that we can model different minds by a common standard. We can dwarf them but not change them; we can hinder men from showing what they are, but we cannot make them otherwise.

"Apart from general human characteristics, each indivdual is born with a distinctive temperament which determines his genuis and character. All characters are good and healthy in themselves. Every man has his special place in the order of the universe.

"What results from an education begun from the cradle and always carried out on the same system without regard for the extraordinary differences between human minds? The effect is usually to give children harmful or misplaced instruction, while they are deprived of the teaching which would really have suited them. Their nature is confined on every side; great qualities of mind are destroyed to make room for small, apparent, unreal substitutes. We indiscriminately employ children of different bents in the same exercises; the rest of their education destroys the special bent and the result is a dull uniformity. Then, after we have wasted our efforts in stunting the true gifts of nature, we see the short-lived and illusory brilliance which we have substituted die away, while the natural abilities which we have crushed never revive. We find these little prodigies all becoming men without power or merit, noticeable only for their uselessness and weakness. Plato, what is your reaction?" Rousseau had addressed the silent newcomer. Still a bit perplexed by the company he was in, Pete tried to be attentive as Plato began.

"To educate those who are different, it is necessary for you to recognize these facts: The most important kind of knowledge which the activity of reason can yield is wisdom; this is knowledge of goodness and of those ways of acting which make up the good life for the individual. The degree to which one can acquire wisdom varies from one person to another. Some are capable of reasoning well, and consequently, apt for the acquisition of knowledge and wisdom. Others possess a low capacity for reasoning but a high capacity for forceful action; they are able through the dominance of spirit to control appetites forcefully, and they will order these well so long as others direct them in the paths of wisdom. Still others possess little reason and little spirit, their souls being con-stituted predominantly by the power to desire. In them the appetites are in the ascendency. They are peculiarly fit for those actions

which lead to the satisfaction of desires. Since the faculties vary
from one person to another, the economic and professional apti-
tudes of each also vary.

"Of course, we must emphasize that I have been around for
more than 2400 years, so people on earth might all be alike by
now. Although, the ones who have been coming here have surely
been different. In all my time around here I've never known two
who are alike."

"Right! Pardon me for interrupting, but I've been listening to
this whole discussion and I can't resist entering the conversation.
I'm a psychometrician and I'd love to put together the research
that will test the hypothesis you people are apparently formulating.
What a study." He stood up in a dazed exultation and moved
unconsciously toward the door. A look of rapture had the man
spellbound as he began to chant. "We'll control the absolute
variables precisely. Then throw figures in computers once or
twicely—

> I'll build a normal curve,
> Then find a mode,
> Plus standard deviations and a mean.
> Next a chi square chart,
> A tendency part,
> And add percentile ranks in between.
> Calculate the distributions on a frequency graph,
> And normal probability too,
> A scattergram with correlations,
> Coefficient demonstrations,
> Yield regression and prediction that is true.
> T scores and Z scores,
> Scaling items right,
> I'll bring reliability to this;
> Difference, contingency, relating chi to phi,
> Multiple regression is a sight,
> Oh pass me the tables, significant at .05,
> So long fellows, I'm better than alive."

"That man does this every time he comes in here," said Dewey
when the statistician had disappeared. "He's always going to start
a research program. Just before he came here he had fifteen grants
going at Validity U. He's never gotten over the fact that he was

never able to complete the research for any of them and his subordinates are living off of that grant money. All of this attention to the categorizing of people reminds me of the way we use to weigh pigs in Vermont. We'd put a board across a fence, balancing the board at right angles to the fence. After placing the pig on one end of the board, we stacked rocks on the other end until the pig and the rocks seemed to strike a balance. Then we'd guess how much the rocks weighed, and that became the accurate weight of the pig."

Pete questioned himself and others by asking, "Is it probable that these categorizing efforts cause us to focus on the wrong concern? I begin to feel that trying to isolate certain students as different is, in effect, a stifling conception of curriculum development and instructional behavior. What is your reaction, Maria?"

Maria Montessori seemed to welcome the invitation to release her intense feelings on this matter. "Pete, I believe stifling is an important word in describing the effects of this quest on what to do when they are different. We are addressing ourselves to a mythical question. If we must answer the question, I say that when they are different, liberate them. The fundamental principle of scientific pedagogy must be, indeed, the liberty of the pupil. We cannot know the consequences of suffocating a spontaneous action at the time when a child is just beginning to be active. Perhaps we suffocate life itself."

"This certainly makes sense to me, Maria," Dewey began, his words emerging as something of a verbalized contemplation. "I'm in agreement with our friend Whitehead on this point. Education is life itself, so long as the living thing continues to grow. Education is growth under favorable conditions; the school is a place where those conditions should be regulated scientifically. That is about all there is to it."

"Ah," Pete grabbed what he thought to be the essence of the comment, "the what to do when they are different must be a continuous constructing and reconstructing of situations that establish favorable conditions for the growth of a particular individual—in this discussion, a different individual.

Socrates again directed the discussion, "It seems to me that there is an obligation to include certain specific elements of this education for a world (or a heaven) of human beings—each one being a different individual. Maria, what will you say?"

"The imperative elements aren't at all profound," Montessori began, "but they represent the differences between the school that educates children who are different and the school that works to destroy the differences in people. If there is a genuine desire to educate those who are different (and this means everyone), then the idiotic schemes for prizes and punishments must be eliminated. Prizes and punishments are, if I may be allowed the expression, the bench of the soul, the instrument of slavery for the spirit. Prize and punishment are incentives toward unnatural or forced effort, and therefore we certainly cannot speak of the natural development of the child in connection with them. The jockey offers a piece of sugar to his horse before jumping into the saddle; the coachman beats his horse that he may respond to the signs given by the reins. And yet neither of these runs so superbly as the free horse of the plains. This, of course, suggests the absolute concept of discipline that must prevail if one would educate the child who is different. Discipline must come through liberty. If discipline is founded on liberty, the discipline itself must necessarily be active. I do not consider an individual disciplined only when he has been rendered as artificially silent as a mute and as immovable as a paralytic. He is an individual annihilated, not disciplined. To educate people who are different, it is essential that they be liberated —freed to become involved in the learning process."

As Maria Montessori concluded her statement, two men at the bar (one a Jesuit priest) turned their stools and faced the discussants. Other than these people and the bartender, the room was now empty. The priest was first to speak: "Ma'am, permit me to react to what you have said. I presume your experience is limited. My guess is that your work does not go back even to 1900. With experience you'll discover that students who are different (and these are special cases) cannot be given much liberty. They must be governed by specific policies and regulations. I am Father Manare. My friend, a man who agrees with me, is E. W. Scripps. He amasssed a fortune in the newspaper business. I doubt if he did this by liberating incompetent employees. Your comments, Miss Montessori, remind me of a Jesuit school I inspected in Germany in 1580. The place lacked conformity and discipline in that the boys had not been told how they were to conduct themselves. I corrected this easily by issuing a directive to the boys at the conclusion of my inspection. I told the boys that when they go for a walk, they were not to stamp along indecorously like country folk. They should not spit in front of bystanders but turn their heads courteously to one side. If they have to spit in church, they should rub it out with their foot. In the refectory they should not gobble nor splash the gravy about nor blow their noses in their napkins. In class they should not chatter among themselves nor laugh at what is said. This, my dear lady, is discipline that keeps the boys in line. It requires a matter-of-fact statement of what is to be."

E. W. Scripps picked up the conversation. "Be diplomatic, but don't be too damned diplomatic. It is rare indeed when circumstances are such that a conscientious man can lose anything by fearless, frank speech and writing."

Pete then asked Scripps, "Sir, shouldn't this actually emphasize the need to liberate the different student so he can participate in the fearless, frank speech and writing you described so well?"

"Hell, boy, you just don't understand." With that absolute by Scripps, the two agreeable partners left the room.

Maria handed Pete a book entitled *Letters to My Teacher*. He read a paragraph she had underlined. "Sometimes the average classroom reminds me of the old Japanese clubbing tournaments: you put ten people in a closed arena and let them beat their brains out until one of them comes out the winner. He is the class valedictorian." "I guess this is the solution Father Manare would have to our problems of what to do when they are different."

Dewey arose from the table and spoke to Pete, "Stay here for a while and contemplate our discussion. The three of us are going out to my place, and we'll expect you to join us when you get hungry. I want to share my site in paradise. It's exactly what I asked for. I'm running an experimental school on 1,000 acres of Vermont-like landscape where the spirit of human-centered experimentation contains the zest of my early years at the University of Chicago and the informal neighborliness of my winter home in Key West. It's different, but exciting. You'll not find two of the teachers alike. And the children? Well, you find out for yourself. They're just different. Socrates must get to a seminar where they are concentrating on the problems of conformity and uniformity among recent candidates for heaven. Drop in anywhere, anytime. We'll find something you'll enjoy."

Pete found himself alone in the bar. The entire spectrum passed through his mind as he savoured the remainder of the occasion. "If only I could give this speech to all educators on earth and magically create a mood where they would permit themselves to assimilate the message. Five minutes is all I'd need. 'When They Are Different.' I'd say:

> No one is other than a different person.
>
> Difference is the most cherished quality that human beings can have.
>
> Seeing people as other than different subverts the potential of this cherished human quality.
>
> Perceiving all people as inevitably and properly different brings all educational planning into a focus that promotes a dynamic individuality among the total population.
>
> Perhaps I would conclude that 'When They Are Different' means I've finally begun to see when I look."

Pete looked up and into the dazzling eyes of the angelic waitress he had observed earlier. She was dressed magnificiently—but differently. He took her by the hand and the two drifted through the lobby and outside. Dewey and the experimental school could wait. Pete had different ideas.

"To think that this is what I'm to do for an eternity," Pete mused. "Heaven is surely a great place for those who are different."

on special education

I believe the idea of Special Education has evolved to an unfortunate extreme. Certainly a child who is blind requires a special education. This is equally true for the child who is deaf, physically handicapped, or severely mentally retarded. Beyond these categories, I seriously question the desirability of special programs and special teachers for the multitudes of the so-called specializations. By endlessly inventing new classifications in the area of Special Education, the entire endeavor is in serious danger of domination by persons seeking to create an empire for themselves at the expense of children and parents. In this story I have described my concern. It is intended as a caution, a red flag. The excellent people in Special Education are in danger of being subverted by the opportunists who have invaded this vital part of the educational system.

the story of harry and charlotte–
two special people
A Brief Romantic Tragedy

"Can it be ten years since I made the big move? Imagine, I was a junior high school teacher—and a good one, considering the system that was tolerated in those days. Junior high school. I had almost forgotten the term. What was that other division we had in those days? Ah, yes, the elementary school. Funny," Harry mused, "how those relics slip away from a guy. Sometimes I get almost nostalgic over those times. Then I remember the system and realize how far I've brought this town. It was the journal article that spirited me toward stardom as 'Mr. Special' of the educational world. What was the article? Oh, yeah, 'Doctorate or Bust.' That was it. . . . spelled out some alternatives. That's when I plotted my two five-year plans. With my first federal subsidy I went off for doctoral study in Administration and Supervision of Special Education. Did all right, too, with courses in

Introduction to Special Education
Principles of Special Education
Understanding Special Education
Promoting Special Education

. . . those basic courses are really something. I guess it was when we got to the doctoral seminars in Special Education that I really caught fire. Yes, those were enlightening. . . .

Introduction to the Administration of Special Education
Principles of Special Education Administration
Understanding the Administration of Special Education
Grantsmanship and the Administration of Special Education

Techniques for Inflating Staff and Program Needs in Special
   Education
How to Win With the Legislature
Use of Statistics to Build Your Case

H. K. Ree, I must modestly acknowledge, emerged from them a
polished operator."

Arriving at the parking lot, Harry found his reserved spot
occupied. "A few years before and I would have been irate," he
reflected, "but I've become quite magnanimous since my position
is stable. That car in my usual place has a Washington, D.C.
license. Who might be wanting my time?"

Harry entered the two-story, circular glass structure that was his
headquarters. It always amused him that at last the bank had found
a profitable, long-term occupant for this provocative but function-
less structure. Thank heavens there were ample federal funds for
renovation and revitalizing of the building.

In a manner befitting his executive stature, H. K. responded
coldly to the greeting of his vast secretarial staff and entered the
Danish modern hideaway called his office. With practiced aloofness
he had communicated an unawareness that someone was waiting
in the reception area to see him on Special Education business.
Settled behind walnut, carpeting, and leather (government sur-
plus), H. K. responded to the buzz on his intercom: "Dr. Ree, a
Dr. C. Tann is waiting to see you."

Immediately, H. K. Ree applied his doctoral study to the problem. Gazing at his immaculate, paper-free desk, he replied, "Let
me take care of some urgent paper work and then I'll see Dr.
Tann." Stallmanship, an imperative technique in Special Education, became Harry's immediate reaction. He pulled out several
standby federal grant proposals and scattered them about his
desk. Then he took from his golf bag his favorite putter and
sharpened the old golf game by shooting for a coffee cup placed
at a challenging spot on the carpet. Ten minutes seemed adequate
as the delaying tactic for his unknown visitor. Harry returned to
his desk, adopted the academician's scowl that had carried him
through many situations he construed as requiring a scholarly
facade, and directed the secretary to admit Dr. C. Tann.

The facade collapsed as the visitor entered. "I'm Dr. Tann,
Special Services Director for the United States Office of Special

Education. Let me tell you, Dr. Ree, I've been anticipating this moment ever since I left Washington on our tour of Special Education Centers. You certainly rank high in the central office. You know, since we took over those buildings the former agency occupied, the U.S. Office of Education—too bad we had to dissolve their operation—we've been hearing great things about you and your work. I must say, Dr. Ree, I like what I see."

Harry Ree stuttered, sputtered, couldn't articulate. "Well, Dr. Ree," Charlotte gasped, "I've heard that a high proportion of teachers in Special Education have gravitated to the field because of its relationship to problems in their own life. Are you a product of a speech-handicapped division of Special Education?"

Dr. Charlotte Tann was, to be succinct, H. K. Ree's kind of woman. Immediately her life interfered with the life of Harry, and she did so simply by standing and being. Long, lean, loose, lovely—she created a kind of inner tension in Harry that he customarily identified as a deviate characteristic in a person. He had signed many papers that had endorsed the identification of persons who had these inner tensions as Behavior Deviations. Surely Harry would not become the victim of his own dynasty.

Dr. Tann interfered with his growth processes. She spoke, "Dr. Ree, we regard your program as the exemplification of all we have sought to attain in Special Education. As I understand your attainments, you have eliminated all elementary and secondary schools (in the conventional conception), and you have inserted the diverse categories of Special Education as pertinent replacements. We applaud you from Washington. My motive in being with you is to discover the detailed elements of your triumphs. Soon we could have the Ree National Program of Special Education for All American Youth."

H. K. Ree violently struggled for composure. Dr. Tann had exhibited an animated speech pattern that compounded his dilemma. How would he dissolve those behavioral manifestations? The journal on his desk proved to be the vehicle for conversation.

"Yes, Miss Tann, I'm flattered by your comments and your presence. Let me try to respond to your kind inquiry. The recent journals of exceptional children are fundamental to the inservice programs we maintain. In the past four months these articles have been the discussion of our staff sessions. Let me show you, for example, articles we regarded as exciting for our faculty seminars in Special Education. Of course, we want to express our thanks to you and the U.S. Office for financing our seminars. Having time on week days and aboard our Special Services yacht has set the necessary psychological mood for these professional tasks.

In the past four months we have discussed these articles from the journal:

A HIERARCHY OF COMPETENCIES FOR TEACHERS OF EMOTIONALLY HANDICAPPED CHILDREN

I must confess that none of our experts in this field had these competencies, but what the hell, the sailing weather was perfect. Then we got into the milieu of

A STUDY OF THE EFFECTIVENESS OF MILIEU THERAPY AND LANGUAGE TRAINING FOR THE MENTALLY RETARDED

One of our secretaries put a twist on this idea in a new game called Milieu Therapy. It's kind of reserved for our yacht sessions. I hope you will let me get you involved while you're here. Then came last month's cruise and our study of

THE EFFECT OF RHYTHMIC AND SENSORY MOTOR ACTIVITY PROGRAM ON PERCEPTUAL-MOTOR SPATIAL ABILITIES OF KINDERGARTEN CHILDREN

Frankly, this vital study fit a beat so well that we spent three days and nights dancing to the title. Calypso proved to be the favorite— at the .01 level of significance. Next week we tackle

A DIAGNOSTICALLY BASED CURRICULUM FOR PSYCHOSOCIALLY DEPRIVED PRESCHOOL, MENTALLY RETARDED CHILDREN! INTERIM REPORT

from the latest journal issue. We have a little contest going to see who can come up with the largest number of candidates for his curriculum. The winner gets this month's $1,000 bonus from the new stimulation grant we won in a run-off with three cities."

"Dr. Ree," Charlotte whispered, "these words arouse something within me that I fail to understand. What's happening to me? Tell me more."

"Well, Charlotte—May I call you Charlotte?—what I'm about to show you is in strictest confidence. This promises to revolutionize certain dimensions of our world of Special Education which, as we know, is the only remaining power structure in education." H. K. Ree brought out a stack of papers, reproductions of an article. "The title will describe the nature of my present research emphasis. Here! This is probably my best writing in the field. It will be the lead article in *Esquire, Playboy,* and several other professional journals, simultaneously. Get this title!

DR. H. K. REE WRITES AGAIN

A PSYCHOLEXICAL DIAGNOSIS OF THE EFFECTIVENESS OF FUNCTIONALLY SIGNIFICANT TERMINOLOGY (A HIERARCHY OF ITEMS RELATIVE TO THEIR INSERVICE SEDUCTIVE CAPABILITY) OF SEXUALLY ADVANTAGED, PSYCHOLOGI-CALLY DEPRIVED, EMOTIONALLY CHARGED, PERCEPTU-ALLY HANDICAPPED, SEXY, SPECIAL EDUCATION TEACHERS: AN INTERIM, ACTION RESEARCH OVERVIEW WITH IMPLICATIONS FOR FURTHER RESEARCH!"

Charlotte was properly awed by the stimulating quality of Harry's scholarship. At any rate Harry perceived this in her re-sponse. Now H. K. Ree became anxious—emotional. His voice trembled with lust. He couldn't determine whether it was his lust for Special Education power or for Charlotte. Perhaps there is a difference. "Must be researched," he pondered. Fortunately, trans-fer of training occurred. Dr. Ree utilized his work in that great course, Remediation of Emotional Responses in the Adult Male. He prescribed for himself both an involvement with his professional tasks and an involvement with Charlotte—in that order.

"Char—Do you mind if I call you Char?—here's the key to my attainments—the line and staff organization." He guided Charlotte to the embossed, framed chart on his paneled office wall. Yes, he was sure that her perfume selection was his favorite for this type of woman—"Joy." The fragrance clinched his Special Education plans for the day.

"You'll notice that everyone is directly responsible to me. I am the control. The result is that they expect me all the time but never know when I'll arrive. The anxiety produced by this scheme puts a few on edge, but I maintain that anxiety is a fruitful professional condition."

"And what is this?" Charlotte pointed to a gold-framed citation. As she pointed, she turned and gazed warmly into the Intellectually Gifted eyes of Dr. Ree. He said nothing but fixed his distraught expression on Charlotte's magnetic loveliness. She continued, "Dr. Ree, do you have an Auditory Handicap?"

The magic jargon brought him back to Special Education, somewhat. "No . . . not at all. The Citation? Let me show you. Read it aloud."

Charlotte read from the elaborate scroll:

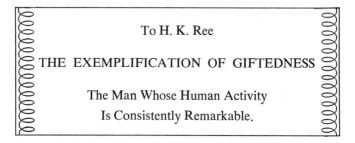

To H. K. Ree

THE EXEMPLIFICATION OF GIFTEDNESS

The Man Whose Human Activity

Is Consistently Remarkable.

Harry concentrated on Charlotte as she read. This time he diagnosed her profile. He saw in Charlotte Tann a potentially valuable line of human activity. How could one woman possess such obvious giftedness? He took Charlotte's hand and led her to the Special Education sofa. Using the remote unit attached to an adjoining table, Harry employed technology to electronically close the velvet draperies, open a panel containing a movie screen, automatically set up a movie projector, and darken the room.

"This film will take you on a tour of the community and show you our Special-Special Education Centers." Charlotte leaned her "Joy" fragrant head on Harry's shoulder. He gasped with the joy of "Joy" and Charlotte and stammered through a narration of the film.

"That was once called Riverside High School. Now it is the Special Education Center for the Intellectually Gifted. It contains separate programs for each of the gifted-child pressure groups. There is one for the 110 I.Q. bunch, the 120 group, a 130 program, a 140, and an Others group. Each group discredits the other, but it makes more of a ferment in the setting. This was Mayfield Elementary in the old days. Now it is our Behavior Disorders Center. Now you are looking at what was Eastgate Elementary. Now it's the Speech Handicapped Center."

Charlotte interrupted. "Who are those adults around the different buildings playing volleyball and sunbathing?"

"Well," Harry reacted, "those people were classroom teachers in the old days. We retrain a few, but most of them live off our Accommodation Grant that makes it possible for these people to stay around until retirement in ten or twenty years. It was an excellent piece of expedience legislation."

The film took an hour to run, but from it Charlotte received a thorough insight into the specific sites of the many Centers. In this county the transition to Special Education was utopian in its completeness.

Harry returned the slide projector and, again, with his electronic marvel, turned on the proper music and delivered pre-lunch martinis. Since both were, by professional commitment, others-oriented, the ensuing embrace brought Charlotte and Harry into a warm, communicating, rewarding, vibrant interpersonal relationship. It contained everything that specialists might envision for such a circumstance.

Eventually Harry managed to whisper, "Charlotte your human activity is consistently remarkable. I feel strong inner tensions. My emotions are disturbed."

"But Harry," Charlotte said, "this behavior could have a detrimental effect on your development and adjustment. Are you a Behavior Deviation?"

"Oh hell, Char, my anxieties are damn sure apparent." In that situation Dr. Tann demonstrated her giftedness in Social Leadership. A remarkably valuable line of human activity, say the experts in Special Education. Giftedness personified was Charlotte Tann.

The remainder of the day and evening found Harry K. Ree and Charlotte Tann deeply involved in highly personalized Special Education. The sessions terminated at 3:00 A.M. when Harry found his way back to his apartment.

Exhausted, but unable to sleep, possibly categorized in Special Education as a Special Health Problem, Harry picked up the newspaper. The article he read described a boy who, after the careful diagnosis of specialists, had spent twelve years in a school for the mentally retarded only to have doctors now discover that he is a genius who has a hearing impairment. Harry threw the paper aside and picked up a magazine. He read of a young man, an outstanding scholar, who flunked out of college. The student revolted against society and moved into New York's lower East Side. He acquired a tremendous respect for the enormous intensity in the lives of persons with whom he lived. "Behavior Deviations," Harry concluded. Then he read on. The article revealed that the young man has become deeply involved in creating new music and film ideas. His work has been featured at Lincoln Center in New York City. Harry closed the magazine and turned to his bookcase. An old book somehow caught his eye. *Dibs—In Search of Self*. Harry smiled as he recalled how it had once influenced his thinking. Then he became disturbed at how far he had gone in the opposite direction. Conscience appeared in his behavior for the first time in many years. He fell into a restless sleep that was punctuated with nightmarish flashes of research data he had long discarded. These ideas appeared to him almost like neon signs in the night.

Research has shown that:

Nurses who display a qualitative bedside manner in their early years of nursing tend to lose this essential quality after some years in the profession.

Master Degree candidates in Guidance display a strong "others-orientation" when they begin graduate study and reveal far less of this characteristic when they finish a Master's Degree in Guidance.

Parkinson's Law demonstrates that the creation of one position soon creates a multiplication of subordinate positions and new diffusions of function.

An effective teacher, one sensitive to children's individuality, is a more influential factor than the grouping scheme devised.

All the children in the school have a gift, and it is the school's responsibility to identify it and do something about it.

I.Q. scores are not static. With appropriate elements in one's education, many persons' I.Q. scores can be raised more than twenty points.

Harry awoke suddenly, dripping with perspiration. What had he done? The empire he had so carefully established seemed to have become a farce. He showered, dressed, and hurried to his office. The Washington car was again in his place and it was only 8:00 a.m. Ree burst into his office, anxious to begin atoning for the monstrosity he had designed.

Abruptly he stopped. Charlotte was sitting at his desk busily shuffling grant proposals.

"Dr. Ree," she began, "it is unfortunate for you, but I have replaced you in this position as Director. Our conversations yesterday were taped and flown to Washington. They have been carefully studied, and we conclude that you are totally incompetent. Diagnosing your behavior with what we know from the literature, your condition is defective in the following Special Education categories. You are a Behavior Deviant (both socially and emotionally maladjusted), Speech Handicapped (stuttering, articulating disorders, delayed speech), Visually Handicapped, Auditory Handicapped, and have Special Health Problems. You clearly evidenced these yesterday.

"You may leave now. Your personal belongings will be sent to your apartment.

"You will be interested to learn that our concentration in the immediate future will be in teacher education. For example, you have general specialists in the area of gifted. If you were up on the literature, you would know that we must have special training for teachers of Disadvantaged Gifted Children, Advantaged Gifted Children, Tall Gifted Children, Small Gifted Children. . . ."

Dr. Tann's voice trailed off as Harry left the office. He wandered down to the yacht and entered the cabin—totally beaten.

"How could I have been so blind. She's so lovely. So gifted. Dr. C. Tann. Charlotte. Charlotte Tann. Charlotte Tann."

A few drinks caused him to slur a bit as he repeated her name: "Charlotte Tann . . . Charlottetann . . . Charlatan . . . CHARLATAN! Of course! How could I have been so stupid?"

Charlotte sat triumphant at the desk and contemplated the name plate. . . .

Dr. H. K. Ree

"Harry K. Ree . . . not a bad guy," she thought. "Stupid, but all right. Harry K. Ree. . . . Good heavens!" she screamed. "This can't be."

Charlotte ran from the office and went directly to the yacht, assuming this would be the refuge for Harry's spirits. She ran to the ship's cabin and saw what must have been inevitable. A specialist to the end . . . Harry K. Ree. Yes, he had gone out in the style of his title. In disgrace, Harry K. Ree had to choose Harikari as the only noble alternative.

Charlotte Tann mournfully assumed control of the empire. As a specialist of many gifts, it would be a long time before another charlatan could dethrone Charlotte Tann.

encouragement for the
venturesome

from deodorant to pizzazz

School as it is conventionally practiced represents the very antithesis of quality in human development. Somehow the reasons why schools were created in the first place seem to have paled to insignificance. Any school can become the arena for bringing quality to the lives of people. Money is a delightful peripheral element for embellishing a circumstance that is designed for educating. Unfortunately, lack of money has become the excuse for poor educational practices when in fact it is no more than a splendid embellishment.

By grabbing hold of the raw materials for educating, it is possible to establish a beautiful learning situation. What are the raw materials for education? They are people who call themselves teachers, a place (that may or may not be what is characteristically called a school), learners (regardless of their chronological ages), and time.

The game then becomes identifying what needs to be done with the learners to help them grow, what talent is available among the teaching population, how space will be used to enhance what educators have identified as needing to be done with the learners, and how to use time as an open-ended element. Within this context, I repeat George B. Leonard's idea, "there are no neutral moments." People are constantly growing intellectually, either positively or negatively. Either good things are happening or bad things are happening. Intellectually there are no plateaus. Teacher talents, spaces, and time are being used on the learners. Since there are no neutral moments, and the whole business is to help learners grow positively, how well does a given situation pass the test? Is it making a positive or a negative contribution to the lives of the learners?

Endless collections of curriculum guides, handbooks, lesson plans, textbooks, and phoney field experiences have successfully subverted school types of education. The world of ideas is bursting out all over the place but not in the organized schemes of the school. Alternatives are simple and available. Implementing the alternatives breeds excitement and quality in teaching, but a special personal savvy is required to make the alternatives go. Not every teacher can permit himself to come alive and organize a way of life with learners that is fruitful for all involved.

Solutions cannot be found by waiting for a school-wide, system-wide, or even course-wide subscription to what might be. An individual teacher simply cannot and should not wait for total faculty endorsement before moving ahead into a way of life in education that has verve and vitality. If an individual teacher finds a partner who can become turned on about an idea, this is a bonus, and the two of them can proceed. If five teachers in a school can become a team with vision and a free-swinging conception of learner involvement, this is almost a miracle, and it can be parlayed into a fabulous experience.

Don't wait for nirvana. You might already be there. The perfect life is experienced in spurts and moments. By grabbing hold of every possibility and moving ahead with an idea, even if it is an individual teacher with a group of learners, one can have that moment that could be the essence of nirvana.

By seizing the circumstance and proceeding with a moment of education that fits the description of the so-called "happening," both teacher and learner have become oblivious to those external realities that convince too many of us that it can't be done. "Yes, but" is still the mightiest sword for the status quo. It continues to be the handiest acceptable reason for sustaining a brand of school experience that makes a negative difference in the lives of the learners. This is why schools continue to be organized into departments and subjects. The vested interest crowd is always an amazing phenomenon, and it reaches its highest level in school organization.

Because of what we insist on contriving in the schools, learners must bootleg any quality education that occurs in the vicinity. Fortunately, they become very effective bootleggers. A friend of mine was, some years ago, the principal of a junior high school that was located in a rather hard-nosed part of a large city. This fellow is probably the finest teacher I've ever met. He tells a great story about his administrative life. Youngsters who attended the school had discovered long ago that the city is education and school is a place where one goes in between those hours of real education that occurs on the street. One ninth-grade boy had discovered that pinching girls on the bottom was a very rewarding kind of thing to do. Word of his discovery soon was communicated to the teachers who related the message to the principal. Wanting to help this young man change his behavior, the principal called him into his office for a discussion. "Are you, in fact, pinching the girls on the bottom?" the principal asked.

"Yes, sir," the boy responded.

"Well now, son, we just can't have that around here. You are going to have to change your behavior. Now you must remember my boy that this can't go on." Then the principal gave the socially appropriate final comment, "I want you to realize that these young ladies just don't like it when you pinch them on the rear end."

The boy spontaneously responded, "Some of them do."

School in this instance became the place where the young man discovered many things about bottom pinching. He learned which girls enjoy being pinched on the bottom. He also discovered that many girls have bottoms that are fun to pinch. What he needed to weigh in his mind was whether to continue his indiscriminate bottom pinching and simply depend on a high percentage of successes or to be more selective and continue to pinch the bottoms of those girls who seemed to enjoy the attention. It would probably be difficult to find many teachers who would have bottom pinching in the lesson plan. Certainly the process of writing a multiple choice test on bottom-pinching insights would demand some skills in constructing test items that few teachers possess. It is probably safe to assume, however, that if such a unit were put into a teacher's lesson plan, that teacher would figure out a way to have right and wrong answers and a normal curve on bottom pinching. Surely it would have to be called the normal curve on the normal curve.

The gamut of planning school experience is essentially based on whatever sin list or value list a particular teacher brings to the planning process. Because the teacher cannot be bothered with a great deal of looking, the curriculum becomes blind adherence to a course of study or a textbook.

Many years ago on the Jack Benny radio program, Phil Harris was the band leader connected with the show. One night they were doing a skit in which Benny and his friends were trying to get Phil Harris to go out on the town. This was shortly after Phil Harris had married the beautiful Alice Faye. After a certain amount of badgering from his friends about an evening with a fresh tomato, Phil Harris responded, "Why should I look all over town for butter when I've got it in the icebox?" This is precisely the problem that exists in identifying significant ways to involve learners with the teacher talent, space, and time they are allotted. The world of ideas is at their fingertips waiting to be utilized in the positive growth of the learners. The formula then is to forget about periods (those capsules of time that fragment a school program), eliminate departments such as English, science, music, and grab hold of the enticing potential of teachers' planning together every day, making decisions about how to use time, space, and people. As a result, the so-called curriculum is tremendously fluid. It takes the form of a high-quality department store where there is an enormous diversity of subject matter and resource people ready and waiting for the learners who enter the marketplace, the world of ideas.

With each new source of money the setting acquires pertinent embellishments. More books, more TV, more telephone contact with the world, vast quantities of audio tapes, increasingly sophisticated immersion with the computer and its possibilities, the Library of Congress on Random Access, a vast library of single-concept films, huge open-carpeted areas containing congenial, comfortable furniture, immediate access to the world via jet, constant involvement of community talent—all or none of these embellishments. The important thing is to see the vision and to start. It is an educational setting that is task oriented and not time oriented. The six weeks' test concept is replaced by the continuous individualized evaluations of positive progress for the individual. It is the school for success. In this setting failure occurs only temporarily as all participants restructure a situation that will generate success. There is no student failure.

Among the many sickly concepts that prevent sensitive teachers from performing imaginatively is the abominable notion of the

"Is this the way you plan to spend your peak learning years?"
Saturday Review   August 22, 1970

unit. The unit is a packaged collection of exercises that drags learners through a dreary number of weeks dealing with some-body's notion of what they ought to learn and how they ought to learn it. Usually the only spice that's engineered for the unit is deleted because it requires going beyond the four walls of the classroom. The student involvement that could come from vast field experiences, from extensive telephone contacts, from personal-ized uses of films and resource people is deleted. So we continue in a system where one teacher has the unit called Eskimos, another Indians, another Rome, and, inevitably, The Hot Wet Lands. The unit concept only serves to narrow the potential for curriculum and to perpetuate an allegiance to right-answer schools.

The unit concept seems comparable to claims of a financially successful deodorant. "Nothing touches you but the spray itself." For the sale of deodorant, this is probably an appropriate slogan. Unfortunately, it more effectively describes what happens to people when they attend school. This description fits "schoolness" regard-less of whether the person is in a kindergarten, a sixth grade, a non-grade, a graduate school, or a Sunday school. School con-tinues to be the place where one goes to be sprayed. In a few moments the spray wears off, revealing the same individual who came to school and who hurries away from the "Right Guard" environment called school to acquire an education on the streets.

The alternative is to create arrangements for an education at school that are pizzazzy. If a man wants to sell whiskey, automo-biles, or shaving cream, he reaches for some pizzazz and he suc-ceeds. Attempts to sell people on an involvement in the world of ideas that could be life in school reject pizzazz because it is assumed to be too flashy, so the deodorant spray style that has little more than a temporary influence on improving the quality of the life of the individual is adopted.

And what is pizzazz? Pizzazz is something extra classy—like the effervescence of fine champagne. If this is applied to a study of what happens in school, I would conclude that there are very few pizzazz-like experiences occurring under the direction of teachers. What a tragedy this is. The tragedy is that there are never any planned experiences in school that students perceive as having the effervescence of fine champagne. Even understanding what I am describing demands an experiential background of education that had to occur outside the school. To envision this extra classy experience, one must have had a direct contact with the effervescence of fine champagne. Perhaps one could acquire this vicariously, but I seriously question the validity of such vicarious perceptions of something extra classy.

In the play "Auntie Mame" there is a delightful line relating to the whole notion of pizzazz. Mame is talking to Patrick, her young nephew, trying to get him to enjoy the good life. She says, "Patrick, life is a banquet, but most poor S.O.B,s are starving to death." Such is the circumstance in school. What makes it more tragic is that the starvation diet we serve up is teacher designed. I guess I am encouraging teachers to follow their notions. They know what a banquet looks like, and they are capable of creating one. Perhaps it needs to be a smorgasbord-type banquet. Instead of the monotony of the traditional curriculum checklist, why not take a retrospective look at each day with students and ask, "Did I use the gentle, temporary, deodorant approach today? If so, I must acknowledge that it will wear off before the youngsters get home. Or did I engineer a day with real pizzazz? Did I lead some learners through something extra classy?"

on communication

enticements to eupsychia

One day I was in the local drugstore in the process of purchasing a few postage stamps from the stamp machine. I dropped a quarter in the slot and bent down slightly to determine which of the three levers I would pull in order to get the stamps I wanted. While in this position, a gentleman came up behind me, reached past my shoulder, and dropped a coin in the stamp machine. I raised up and reached for the lever that would feed me the selected stamps. At that moment the strange gentleman behind me said, "Wait a minute, that's my quarter." I tried to explain that I, too, had put a quarter in the machine and was making a selection. He pushed me aside and said, "That's my quarter." Then he selected his stamps by pulling the appropriate lever.

I said, "Now, let's see if any more come out." So, I pulled the lever again. Another set of stamps came from the machine. I turned to the gentleman and said, "You see, I wouldn't steal your quarter."

Still totally unconvinced, he looked at me and said, "You look like the kind of a guy who would."

I had never seen the man before and I have never seen him since. However, my physical self and pattern of behavior communicated an influential message that directly determined the man's attitude and behavior toward me. What kind of a guy was he? What kind of a person am I insofar as his perceptions are concerned? The problems of interpersonal communication begin before a word is spoken. The communication that is wordless substantially influences a subsequent verbal communication. To bring about change in education, one has no choice but to become competent as a communicator. How does one acquire such a competence?

"HAVE YOUR NEXT AFFAIR HERE." These words were emblazoned upon the marquee of a large hotel I passed while riding in a taxi from the airport to Miami Beach. When I arrived at my hotel, the person I saw in the lobby was a lovely young lady wearing on her extremely attractive dress a button that read, "I AM A PEOPLE PLEASER." What a splendid first impression I received of the area.

Both the sign on the hotel marquee and the sign on the girl were effective. Each communicates its message to enough people and influences behavior to the extent that they can be considered successful communications ventures. The hotel's motive, obviously, was to attract clientele. The young lady's motive?

Both of these communications techniques demonstrate what advertising experts call "controlled obnoxity." The advertiser must successfully appeal to consumers at a level of obnoxity that really attracts them to a commodity. Television advertising is frequently the ultimate illustration of this device for communicating a message so successfully that it directly alters a person's behavior. That is, it rigs the arrangement (via controlled obnoxity) whereby multitudes of viewers are rendered receptive to a product or an idea. A constant hazard is present. At what point does an advertisement cross a magic line beyond which the communication is indeed perceived as obnoxious? What will the traffic bear? When does nausea set in? How much can the learners take and still behave as a given manufacturer wants them to behave? The notion of controlled obnoxity has significance for educators and their constant struggle for improved methods of communication.

Concepts of smart merchandising have direct relevance to the arena of interpersonal relationships, the marketplace for education. "How can I communicate my ideas?" "Why can't I communicate with her?" "It's just a problem of communication." These are the perennial questions and comments by teachers and administrators.

I Never Promised You a Rose Garden, Hannah Green, is a superb novel about a sixteen-year-old girl with severe emotional problems. Deborah, in a thought about a fellow patient in a mental hospital reflects: "Did any two people, even in the Real World, speak the same language." Any communication with any other person will never be interpreted precisely as was intended. The best one can do in communicating is to select a content and method which will maximize the probabilities that one will be minimally misunderstood. Each of us must try to sustain a sensitivity to the fact that what one says or writes and what one communicates will always be a result of the filtering process done by each person who receives some concept of the message. Awareness of this reality is a key to communication.

People seldom do any reflecting about the meaning of words; they only feel them. The role of emotion in communication is fantastic. Hostility, pleasure, cooperation, fear, threat—any and all of these are evoked as a person responds to words according to feeling rather than thinking. Feeling then determines a person's reactions, and the entire communication receives what is an interaction of emotion instead of intellect. Intellect and emotion do not function separately. They are always interdependent. Which one will dominate in a particular communication circumstance?

The notion of "controlled obnoxity" is focused at the *feel* level rather than at the *think* level. "HAVE YOUR NEXT AFFAIR HERE." Hardly an intellectual appeal, but it works insofar as the intended result is concerned.

It is a matter of merchandising, in a very positive, quality sense. Education is in the life-influencing business. It is a high-quality motivation. Teachers must acquire a sophisticated savvy in the art of merchandising an involvement of learners with the world of ideas.

My father was a great salesman. The commodities he sold were not particularly significant as applied to the critical needs of man. He was a wholesale candy salesman and a good one. Occasionally, his successes bothered me because he was capable of selling damn near anything. Many years ago he sold gumdrops in thirty-pound cartons. At that time gumdrops sold for ten cents a pound. A small, rural gas station owner bought a carton of gumdrops and put them on display in his candy case with a sign announcing the price, 10¢/ lb. After one week my dad returned to the station. The carton of gumdrops was almost full. Another week passed—still plenty of gumdrops in the candy case. The proprietor was concerned. He said, "What am I going to do about those damn gumdrops you sold me?"

"They'll sell, just give them a chance," my dad reassured.

Another week passed. Still too many gumdrops. Again, the proprietor of the gas station pleaded for help. "Okay," said my confident dad, "I'll show you how to sell them, but you must do as I say."

"Anything to get rid of them," came the response.

My dad took the entire carton from the candy case and placed it on the counter beside the cash register. He removed the price tag marked 10¢/lb. and replaced it with one that read "SPECIAL —19¢ PER POUND." When we returned one week later, the gumdrops were gone. A sellout. This was merchandising.

A fundamental problem with the educational leader is that he is unwilling to become a merchandiser. An idea man must devote equally as much or more time in developing plans for merchandising his idea as he has spent in innovating and developing it. The commodities basic to teaching are the greatest in the world. They deserve to be effectively merchandised. The term "merchandise" must not be perceived as a negative, wheeler-dealer type of activity. Education is always in need of improvements. Changes required for the change frequently threaten values and vested interests. Consequently, those introducing new ideas to education have no choice but to become expert in merchandising those ideas. It is a type of communication. Involving people in the world of ideas and the evolution of new ideas demands excellence in communication. This communication excellence for involvement, interaction, and interpersonal insight occurs as those who are teachers emerge as authentic human beings. Gimmickry is a basic, requisite tool to use in the process. Conversely, when contrasted with a more vital communications necessity, gimmickry becomes peripheral.

If gimmickry is peripheral, then what is the mainstream to follow toward improved communication among people concerned with education? Structuring our energies in the direction of Eupsychia is the answer. Abraham Maslow describes Eupsychia as a society and culture peopled by self-actualizing human beings. In his superb book, *Toward a Psychology of Being,* he describes the qualities of a self-actualizing person and the characteristics of a psychologically healthy person. Communication between the teachers and students, teachers and teachers, principals and teachers, school boards and parents—any combination of persons—is directly dependent upon the extent to which those involved have progressed toward self-actualization. Maslow describes the self-actualizing person this way:

> An episode or a spurt in which the powers of the person come together in a particularly efficient and intensely enjoyable way, and in which he is more integrated and less split, more open for experience, more idiosyncratic, more perfectly expressive or spontaneous, or fully functioning, more creative, more humorous, more ego-transcending, more independent of his lower needs, etc. He becomes in these episodes more truly himself, more perfectly actualizing his potentialities, closer to the core of his Being.

To become such an individual means evolving, struggling, consciously becoming a psychologically healthy person, and this Maslow categorizes as one who has:

1. superior perception of reality
2. increased acceptance of self, of others and of nature
3. increased spontaneity
4. increase in problem-centering
5. increased detachment and desire for privacy
6. increased autonomy, and resistance to enculturation
7. greater freshness of appreciation, and richness of emotional reaction
8. higher frequency of peak experiences
9. increased identification with the human species
10. changed (the clinician would say, improved) interpersonal relations
11. more democratic character structure
12. greatly increased creativeness
13. certain changes in the value system[1]

Eupsychia is "a society and culture peopled by self-actualizing human beings." Such is the answer to questions concerning interpersonal communication. As each person deliberately struggles to become self-actualizing, he is becoming increasingly skilled in communication. In Eupsychia one can even communicate honestly and effectively with self. I find the Maslow characteristics of a psychologically healthy personality tremendously significant to myself as a kind of "how'm I doin" list against which I can take a

---

[1] Maslow, op. cit., pp. 23–24.

frequent look and make a fresh next step toward self-actualization. Especially pertinent is that Maslow describes the self-actualizing person as one who is being instead of becoming. What are the elements I can consciously permit myself to work on as I move through some years of becoming, to some years of being? It is certain that my friends' (or enemies') ideas about what I should work on and what I believe I can permit myself to work on will frequently (usually) not coincide. I regard this as unimportant. I'm the guy who's in (or out of) the mix insofar as my emergence as a self-actualizing person is concerned. Each bit of new sensitivity and insight takes me a bit closer.

I'm impressed by the principles of perceptual psychology. These pack a special wallop when applied to learning more about interpersonal communications:

> What one does makes sense to the person at the time he does it.
>
> People behave according to their beliefs about reality.
>
> What is a threat to one person might be a challenge to the person sitting beside him.

Rather than ask, "Why does he behave that way? why not ask, "What do I think I know about myself that causes me to react in this way to what i think I see in his behavior? What am I willing to do about it in order for us to communicate with continually increasing effectiveness?" Your message is at stake. You want your life to be influenced favorably. A primary life influencer is your own effectiveness in communicating your ideas. This is a fundamental requisite to educational change of a sort that will favorably influence the lives of learners and, subsequently, the total life in any society.

To develop important ideas for improving education is not enough. The ideas must be paralleled by an understanding of how ideas are communicated plus a zest for using those insights in the many arenas of interpersonal relationships.

Education continues to receive a band-aid treatment for its malfunctioning. What is really necessary is major surgery. We apply the band-aid remedy because educators are a long way from Eupsychia, and so we fail to merchandise our ideas. Perhaps the first inadequacy promotes a second.

Begin the trip to Eupsychia. It's the place where all occupants are immersed in the basic human endeavors of being problem seekers as well as problem solvers, but the quality of communication is such that each person knows of the other, "Amigo, you are good for my ego."

the paradox

can school become
a place for an education?

Sit-ins, teach-ins, drop-outs, push-outs, cry-outs—what new style will the desperate plea take as students beg to have school become a place in which they can get an education? Schooling and education certainly don't mean the same thing. Schools (kindergarten through college) could become centers for the deliberate cultivation of an enlightened citizenry. Unfortunately, they too frequently are centers in which young people are required to participate in little more than an endurance contest. How tragic. Especially so when there is an alternative.

The very special thing about a human being is that he is a learner. Being an insatiable learner is the fantastically distinctive quality that has made man unique for at least 100,000,000 years. No one can prevent man from learning unless a special drug or operation is used to eliminate this astonishing human behavior. Children, youth, adults—all people possess the innate human characteristic, a love for learning.

Equally special in the scheme of human affairs is that each man decides for himself what he will permit himself to learn. What a fortunate aspect of man's nature. *He* selects how he will become involved in the learning process. This being the case, formal schooling is nothing more than a direct effort to influence what each man will permit himself to learn.

What are the results of this effort to prescribe what another person will learn? Simply this: *Often a teacher teaches that which he had not intended to teach.* Why? Everyone knows of the many times he learned something in school that had nothing to do with what the teacher thought he had taught. While enrolled in a history course designed to teach a student to understand the problems of man and his efforts to solve these problems, the student might learn to hate the study of history. History hating probably wasn't in the teacher's lesson plan (even though behavior of some history teachers seems to indicate that history hating is a prime motive in their teaching). Nevertheless, history hating could be exactly what the student learned. This learning isn't usually measured on the six weeks' test of "what we learned."

When this happens it is a temptation to use the student as a scapegoat for poor teaching rather than to take a reflective look at what the teacher did to induce this learning. The teacher gets away with the scapegoating by referring to the students as incorrigible, not college material, delinquent, unmotivated, immoral, immature, or, this year's most fashionable, disadvantaged. With such generalizations a threat to the teacher becomes a justification, and the teacher becomes a candidate for "teacher of the year" honors, the claims to greatness being: "I have been tough." "I raised academic standards." "I scored 600 on the National Teacher Exam." or "I lectured superbly." This is especially true today as we insist on making bookie joints out of schools by labeling, categorizing, and grouping children in ways that tattoo them for life. They learn to conform to their tattoos very well.

Education of all the children of all the people works! The great American experiment of public education for all people has proved to be a phenomenal success. Occasionally a critic of American public education will suggest that European schools are better. This is ridiculous when measured by any yardstick. The fact is that every day finds educators from other countries coming to the United States to study how our fabulous system can work so effectively. The United States' educational system is emulated throughout the world. It is the key ingredient in sustaining our free society.

Now the question becomes, how do we improve upon the greatest system of education in the world? What is the gap between what we aspire to accomplish and what we accomplish. What's wrong with education in America and what can be done about it?

Perhaps the greatest single problem is the idiotic system of grading that is not only accepted, it is advocated as a motivator for learning. Do grades motivate learning? Absolutely! They motivate students to learn how to get good grades. Getting good grades is accomplished by an endless array of devious techniques, and students are masters at beating the system. They have learned well. Of course, the one who does the best job of learning how to get good grades becomes the Class Valedictorian. This person has mastered the art of grade getting. Such a person has learned that an idea is useless unless it earns an "A" grade. The student who is a thinker has an extremely difficult time in this system. It would be interesting to know how many great thinkers are lost from the world of ideas because the educational system places its rewards in favor of the "right answer" to the teacher's question rather than involves the student in scholarly identification of questions and a diligent pursuit of solutions to those critical concerns. Word swallowing, rather than thinking, is the key to payola in school. To earn the coin of the realm (high grades), it is imperative that the student play the game. Then at the end of a grading period his name is announced over the P. A. system as a member of the honor roll—this announcement made by a principal who somehow forgot why the school was built in the first place.

Significant universities in America are leading the way in elimination of the tragic practice of equating grade getting with learning. Cal Tech, perhaps the finest technological university in the nation, has eliminated grades for freshman students. This decision was made after the faculty had spent a year studying reasons why morale among the freshman students had been steadily declining. The consequence has been a general upswing in attendance at voluntary lectures, greater participation in cultural events, and involvement of students in special projects identified as an outgrowth of an interaction between students and professors since the grade-getting motive has been removed. The system of grading is deeply ingrained in American school programs. I suspect few administrators will have the courage to lead schools toward a more educationally palatable style. Too bad for millions of students.

If students were all docile and conforming, the prevalence of "keeping school" instead of teaching would be even more widespread than it is. Occasionally a "troublemaker" will ask: "Why do we have to study this stuff?" The routine answer?

You'd better get this because . . .

it's going to be on the test.

or

you'll need it in life.

or

you'll need it in college.

or

the teacher in the next grade will
expect you to know it.

Using this technique for the entree, teachers serve up the wildest
assortment of "necessary knowledge" one could possibly concoct.
Such indispensable items as the gerund, the War of 1812, *Beowulf*,
and push-ups are always in the collection. If, as a student in some
previous situation, a teacher had a fabulous experience studying
something, it is a great temptation for that teacher to conclude
that every child should have a similar experience. The consequence
is that for twenty-five years every child gets the same unit because he needs to know about the topic "in order to get along in
life."

Obviously, what is taught must be determined by taking a good
look at the kids that walk in the room. This "good look" is of a
professional, diagnostic quality that the competent teacher possesses. Teacher competence includes, first of all, a feeling of
adequacy and self-worth. If the teacher is insecure, frightened,
unhappy, or unhealthy, he has great difficulty in being able to
build a school program around what he discovers about children.
Rejection of self produces an authoritarian, defensive teacher
behavior, and life becomes a hell for children while under the influence of such a person. Finding a teacher with subject matter
competence is the easiest thing in the world. Getting a teacher who
is knowledgeable and is personally able to use this subject matter
effectively is extremely difficult. This is the primary problem in our
systems of mass education.

What a gigantic task is before us in what is called junior and
senior high school education. In most secondary schools today,
the obsolete systems of periods, credits, honor rolls, and stan-
dardizations are the bill of fare. Even with young ladies who are
cheerleaders the effort is to make them identical in every school.

Rather than involve the children in making some choices as to how cheerleading at a particular school can become unique, special and personal, a "cheerleading specialist" is brought in to standardize the process. This standardization goes so far as to have adolescent girls simulate the deep, hoarse voice of mules while discarding their own exciting, adolescent screams that could make the cheering authentic. The same schools will claim to be nurturing creativity even though this prescriptive style used with cheerleading is identical to that the child experiences throughout much of his school day.

Most every child is required to take a diet of math, English, science, social sciences, and physical education. Why? The problems of man have been accentuated by products of this plan. Art, music, philosophy, literature, drama, dance—the aesthetic dimensions of life that promote a humaneness in the decisions man must make—are regarded as incidentals, appendages, electives. Even when students become involved in these as electives they are confronted with selective admissions procedures. Music teachers "screen" students into the band, chorus, rockettes, and orchestra. Art frequently becomes a ritualistic imitation of the teacher. Drama becomes preparing for the performance. Probably ego involvement of the teacher partially explains this. A more adequate explanation is no doubt found in this being a reflection of what Mother and Dad perceive as "it," which is the same as the schooling they had twenty years ago. It is safe.

PTA could help with the problems if PTA would start over. The essential contribution of a PTA must be to improve educational programs in specific schools. The real potential of a PTA is in the actual membership (students, parents, teachers) when persons sit together in small groups and wrestle through decisions on significant educational problems. The old routine of meeting in the cafeteria to hear the treasurer's report, secretary's report, program plans, and who won tonight's lottery on the "room count" for the most parents attending the meeting simply doesn't change anything or get people deeply involved. Any school can establish and succeed with small-group sessions involving parents, teachers, and students. The superb parents and interested teachers in any school-community should follow their own notions and speak out for what they perceive as valuable for PTA. Looking to conformity with national PTA prescriptions can hardly be the answer. Parents and teachers must meet because there is a personalized reason to meet—not because a minimum number of sessions must be conducted to satisfy requirements of a regional or national edict. Local parents and teachers will make wise choices for sessions designed to improve, extend, or understand educational programs for their children. If parents were involved in seminar-type sessions on educational problems influencing their children, there would soon be a disappearance of such money-making projects as the annual school carnival and the monthly "room count" at formal meetings.

A successful manufacturing concern boasts: "Progress is Our Most Important Product." It is strange that suggestions for progress in education are construed as ridiculous or subversive. Progress in education occurs when parents, students, administrators, teachers—the school community—become involved in a continuous thinking and rethinking of what a specific school is trying to accomplish and the appropriate style of school program for attaining its objectives. The consequence is the creation of sensational school programs.

What are some of the consequences that would be categorized as senational?

A shift from rewarding word swallowing to esteeming idea involvement.

Schools would become places where every child experiences a prolonged (twelve years at least) immersion in an environment that is warm, encouraging, and nonauthoritarian. The beatings disappear, whether they are of the board and bottom type or the more deadly verbal lashings so commonly used. A secondary school Dean who still uses the paddle is simply a dreamer who has not discovered that his idealistic scheme for acquiring blind obedience produces a behavior directly opposite to that sought by his quick-cure technique.

Students escape the deadly consequences of being labeled as slow, remedial, average, stupid. Progress will be a total realization of individualized learning experiences—the only way anyone learns anyway. This is an attainable objective. It is being done in many places where teachers and administrators have permitted themselves to become involved in fresh, exciting new styles of school organization. New style does not mean a retrogression to

"Take advantage of every opportunity to enjoy yourself before you get into kindergarten, Brian. That's when they start breathing down your neck."

Saturday Review   March 7, 1970

departmentalization and homogeneous grouping—styles of organization that simply haven't worked in terms of the objectives
of American education. More money and space and teachers will,
of course, be highly important to this kind of progress. Far more
important, however, is for us to stop repeating the mistakes of the
last one hundred years.

Technology has not reached the student in school in ways that
complement objectives of the school. Television, for example, has
phenomenal potential for individualized learning. So far it has been
used primarily as a tool for expanding the use of a limited instructional technique—the mass consumption of a body of knowledge. Soon every school must afford a self-contained video tape
unit that can bring student involvement into the utilization of
television as a vehicle for self-understanding, for learning to communicate, for action research into significant problems, for utilization of resource people in the community or world, and for an
endless listing of imaginative possibilities. Portable television re-
cording units are instructional necessities for personalizing mass
education.

The Talking Typewriter is an intriguing idea for teaching many
things—especially reading. Failure is virtually impossible with this
electronic innovation. Social sciences, mathematics, music, and
science can certainly be taught with the Talking Typewriter.

The computer has enormous potential. Using it to calculate
attendance or to figure master schedules merely employs a fabulous
device to perform an obsolete task. The computer can add im-
measurably to a personalized educational program if we "ask" the
computer for answers to personalized educational problems such
as specific skills.

Independent study works for many students. Certainly the
choice for independent study should not be made in terms of
whether or not a student makes "A" grades, for an "A" student
might not be one who profits from independent study. The choices
must be made in terms of what one is trying to accomplish at a
specific time—with specific students—not as a reward for a particular learning situation.

What will the result of all this be? No more schools composed
of rectangular boxes, each containing an average of 37.5 children
sitting passively in rows of uncomfortable, straitjacket desks.

An open-ended school will be the way of life. When a teacher asks: "Johnny, what are you doing?" he will respond, "Thinking." The teacher in this setting will never be heard to counter by saying: "Stop thinking and get back to your work." No . . . the teacher will shout: "Great! You are at your proper task." Johnny will be dealing with the new in experience. He will be getting an education . . . in school.

school-an obsolete notion

There are some terrific ideas around that can cause schools to become splendid places for helping children grow. The ideas would not scare people, but the words used in describing them surely would. It's strange how we insist on deterring the growth of children by retaining obsolete arrangements for educating. Sound, fresh ideas are subverted because people are victimized by their own reactions to words. Why? People never think of the meaning of words; they only feel them.

There is a strange mystique about schoolness. Perhaps it is connected with a kind of nostalgia. I wonder sometimes if it is also connected with a reality that a great many people don't believe in freedom. Maybe it's connected to the notion that people tend to hate in others those things they hate about themselves. Maybe it's fear. Woodrow Wilson is supposed to have said that the purpose of a university is to make a child as much unlike his father as possible. When education works, a child emerges quite different from his father. Daddy's ego, therefore, is threatened by an educational idea that he construes as causing his child to acquire a value system different from his. This might be the reason why he would, consciously or subconsciously, feel negatively about words that describe an educational system of a different flavor. Maybe we have to accept the reality that Daddy and Mother don't want education to work. Therefore, they insist upon the perpetuation of arrangements for educating that are essentially a waste of time.

In a recent chat with an assistant superintendent of schools I heard these comments: "In the past five years we have increased teacher salaries substantially, reduced the student-teacher ratio extensively, spent hundreds of thousands of dollars on materials, constructed several new school buildings, increased our number of teachers with master's degrees, and acquired additional guidance counsellors. In the same number of years our number of failures (those receiving F grades) has increased substantially. What teachers describe as discipline problems have increased. The number of dropouts has not decreased. Overall reading achievement scores have gone down. Destruction of school property has increased. I am going to do something about this," he went on to say, "or I will resign. Next year I am leaving this office and reopening an abandoned school in the inner-city section of our community. I am asking the Board of Education for the same per pupil expenditure that exists in our system for any other school, but I am insisting on permission to expend these monies in a totally new way. I am putting my reputation on the line. I guarantee to reverse all of those statistics insofar as the children who attend this school are concerned. If I don't, I will resign. We will have children from ages four to eighteen, an entirely new mix for education, and I promise that we will succeed."

Teaching As a Subversive Activity, a delightful book by Charles Weingartner and Neil Postman, puts it this way: "The American School system is sick. Its methods are based on fear, coercion, and rote-memory testing. What is more, the subject matter it teaches becomes obsolete almost as it is taught: The 'knowledge explosion' demands that students learn how to use their minds and talents while the schools are strenuously engaged in teaching them how to stifle their intelligence and creativity."

Debating the controversy is no longer of any interest to me. School is a bust! As it is conventionally fashioned in periods, modules, middle schools, departments, and courses of study—the entire mess simply doesn't do what it purports to do.

What's the motive of education? In describing his world game, Buckminster Fuller says: "The objective is to work out ways of how to make humanity a continuing success at the earliest possible moment." Or, as Harold Taylor says, "the objective is to help people learn how to make the world work."

What kinds of people will figure out how to make the world work? They are people from Eupsychia. Eupsychia is a world populated by self-actualizing people. People learn to be self-actualizing.

The story of self-actualization is potentially significant for every-one. Everyone should permit himself to study Abraham Maslow's book, *Toward a Psychology of Being*. It is a fantastic experience. Self-actualization, says Maslow, is:

> Ongoing actualization of potentials, capacities and talents, as fulfillment of mission (or call, fate, destiny, or vocation), as a fuller knowledge of, and acceptance of, the person's own intrinsic nature, as an unceasing trend toward unity, integra-tion or synergy within the person.[1]

Self-actualization is a great thing. *The mandate for education is to pattern an arrangement in which a steadily increasing propor-tion of the population will emerge as self-actualizing people.* Any-thing less is subversive to humanity.

This means that each day, each moment in the education setting must be geared to making good things happen to people as an end for that day and that moment.

"Man is made to live, not to prepare to live." Pasternak put those words together in Dr. Zhivago. They describe what education must be.

Education is life—school is anti-life. Teachers continue to make such anti-life comments as "You'd better get this because you're going to need it in the sixth grade." Or the twelfth-grade English teacher says, "You'd better get this because you're going to need it when you get to college." Or, "You'd better get this, you're going to need it in life." What the student needs is not what someone thinks he's going to need someday. He needs what he perceives as significant for himself today. He is living. His education should be geared to his life and the life around him. We continue to im-plement a mythical equation. The equation looks like this:

> textbooks
> recitations
> teacher's questions
> teacher's answers
> grades
> + credits

$$\text{(Sum)} \times \text{Multiple Choice Examinations} = \text{Education}$$

---

[1] Maslow, op. cit., p 23.

The Greek word from which we have derived our word school means leisure. But the prevailing style in school is the antithesis of leisure. Perhaps leisure has a sinful connotation to parents and teachers. "Work for the night is coming" remains a menu for the multitudes. If a child is found in a moment of leisure, leisure in a very quality sense, he will in all probability be told to get back to his work or be sent to the office for having been incorrigible.

The systems for dealing with what a teacher construes as incorrigibility in school have become unbelievably intricate and anti-child. I know of a secondary school that maintains two sets of cumulative folders in the office. Students who are in the O.K. category have a green label on their folders. If a student is sent to the office for incorrigibility, he is given so many points depending on the nature of his crime. Swearing in class, talking back to the teacher, or chewing gum are all categories of incorrigibility, each receiving a different number of points. Upon accumulating an established number of points, the label on the child's cumulative record is changed from green to pink, and he is referred to juvenile court. In this school, therefore, it is literally true that a child can be referred to juvenile court for an accumulation of gum-chewing episodes. He goes to the same court as would a child arrested for stealing a car. Such a system is not rare in our secondary schools.

Only a month ago I entered the central office of a secondary school and approached the reception counter that separates incoming customers from secretaries, administrators, and deans. A large sign was on the counter with this message written in four inch letters:

TIME WILL PASS—WILL YOU?

It was a failure-oriented environment. What was needed? A fundamental reversal of the life style, to be characterized by the removal of the existing sign and replaced by a sign that would read:

GLUNK HIGH SCHOOL—WHERE EVERYONE SUCCEEDS

Success is a good thing for people. The disastrous disease of categorizing, grading, labeling, and failing are in complete violation of plans that produce self-actualizing people. They are the opposite route from Eupsychia.

Carl Menninger wrote effectively in *The Crime of Punishment* about how the "good guys" have an insatiable yen for vengeance.

Those who inhabit our schools as teachers, deans, guidance counsellors, and administrators seem to possess this yen for vengeance
as much or more than people in many areas of endeavor that are
other than people oriented. Perhaps that's why we gravitate to
teaching. Why? One fabulous line, not my own, may be the explanation:

An adult can never educate beyond his own complexes.

What a line! Each of us walks into a situation with other people
as little more than a collection of complexes packaged in some
skin and bones. These complexes then call the tune for how we
react to people and circumstances. This is where the yen for
vengeance takes over. This determines who and when we scapegoat. Our package of complexes determines what brand of hairdo
will bug us, what combination of words will be our irritation or
our flattery, what situation will become the arena for threat, what
will promote fear or reassurance. I believe the essence of teacher
education is the process of becoming sensitive to our own complexes and how they influence our behavior.

Beating children is intolerable. A beating is a beating even
though we might prefer to call it a spanking, a whipping, or a
licking. One person will beat a child and the next day say, "I did
the right thing for him." Another person, after having beaten a
child, will get hold of himself and say something like this: "He
got to me. At the moment I couldn't take it any longer and I
behaved in a way that I know is wrong. I should not have beaten
the child and I must struggle to do better. There will be another
time when I will behave badly but I must continue the struggle of
behaving in ways that I know are good for the child. He got to my
complexes." What a difference there is in the two behaviors. One is
ignorant, defending his ignorance. The other is an enlightened person, both humane and human. He behaved badly but was sensitive
to his error. He is on the road to wisdom, even though he, or any
other person, may never reach the ultimate destination.

All of this paints a picture of conventional schools as obsolete.
Excellent alternatives to school exist. The world today is a fabulous
place in which to live. We are increasingly aware that the world is
the curriculum. The world is made up of cultures, and the cultures
of the world are the basic subject matter for education. But this
does not imply dealing with the cultures in the abstract. It means

seeing them, participating in them. Such a participation is feasible economically, academically, and organizationally on a mass scale.

Involvement of a whole new population of teacher talent is imperative. The artist, the architect, the mechanic, the mother, the writer, the accountant, the sales clerk, the secretary, the postman, the bricklayer, the musician—these are all pieces of teacher talent waiting to be utilized. Such a concept eliminates the ridiculous term "teacher aide." The talented, self-accepting people of society are teachers in the highest quality sense, but self-acceptance is an extremely potent, essential element. The arenas for education are the operational headquarters for each of these people.

Much has been done with the conversion of abandoned stores into centers of education. Organization of the storefront learning centers has resisted the rigidities of the curriculum guide, chalk-board, and desk. Such rigidities are intrusions on education and must be replaced by human beings who can be consistently warm, encouraging, and nonauthoritarian. The culture is the curriculum.

Similarly, furnishings have become inviting, nonthreatening, and casual. The humanities have acquired a central position. Drama has been recognized as a fundamental way to help people grow. Art and music on both a participant and spectator basis have found their appropriate roles of top priority in time and money. These gentle endeavors have brought a magnificent new focus on what is indeed fundamental. Through photography and television students have been involved in fresh approaches to communication in which they literally produce, direct, and film their own ideas of both a creative and documentary sort. They have become active producers of new knowledge rather than passive consumers of old knowledge.

At last the enlightened centers for education have escaped their own boxes. The ingredients are time, talent, space, the world of ideas, and learners. Grades have received their proper burial. The achievement motive is nurtured through threat-free interactions of people.

Having acknowledged that school in the conventional sense is a total bust and having seen many beautiful new patterns emerging, optimism about the future of education in many bright, new forms at last appears. The honeymoon for anti-child school situations is drawing to a close. Access to the world of ideas, people, and things spells out the exciting, attainable future.